D0754340

FIELD OF SCHEMES

How the Great Stadium Swindle Turns Public Money Into Private Profit

JOANNA CAGAN AND
NEIL DEMAUSE

Library of Congress Cataloging-in Publication Data

Cagan, Joanna.
   Field of schemes: how the great stadium swindle turns public
money into private profit / Joanna Cagan and Neil deMause.
         p. cm.
   Includes index.
   ISBN 1-56751-138-4. — ISBN 1-56751-139-2 (lib.bdg.)
   1. Stadiums—United States—Finance. 2. Sports facilities—
United States—Finance. 3. Sports and state—United States. I.
deMause, Neil. II. Title.
GV415.C34 1998
796'.06'873—dc21   97-48625
                                                                 CIP

Common Courage Press
Box 702
Monroe, ME 04951

207-525-0900 fax: 207-525-3068
email: comcour@agate.net

First Printing

TABLE OF CONTENTS

INTRODUCTION: THE VIEW FROM THE CHEAP SEATS

Back in the dim, distant past, when the earth was new and the Carolina Hurricanes were still the Hartford Whalers, we knew little about the world of sports franchise roulette. We probably were about as informed as any regular newspaper reader or ESPN junkie—namely, we knew that sports teams seemed to be moving to new cities, or at least threatening to do so, at an alarming pace. Those that stayed put were more often than not rewarded with new sports palaces with odd corporate names like the TWA Dome and the Pepsi Center. We might have wondered, too, whether these new sports facilities were really worth the hundreds of millions of public dollars being spent on them. And we might have questioned, in idle conversation, the wisdom of spending such exorbitant amounts of money on behalf of private interests while so much of what we knew and loved about U.S. cities was falling apart.

Mostly, all we knew back then, in the fall of 1995, was that the Cleveland Browns were no more.

Each of us had a long history as a sports fan. Joanna grew up in Cleveland, singing the Browns Christmas song in 6th grade choir and generally confident in the notion that football and

Sunday afternoons would forever go together. The announcement in November 1995 that longtime owner Art Modell was yanking the team away to Baltimore stunned locals. If this could happen to one of the most devoted fan bases in the country, it could happen anywhere.

Suddenly, the topic of team relocation and stadium construction seemed to deserve greater scrutiny. Local taxpayers had handed over hundreds of millions of dollars for a new baseball stadium for the Indians—should they have done the same for the Browns? And at what point was it fair for a beleaguered populace, facing a neglected educational infrastructure and a continued urban exodus, to say enough is enough, we deserve to have sports teams *and* a successful school system?

For Neil, meanwhile, growing up a Yankee fan meant riding the subway to the newly renovated ballyard in the Bronx 30 times a year, to sit in $1.50 bleacher seats with a crowd more diverse than you'd find most anywhere in a rapidly polarizing city: Latino families from the surrounding neighborhoods, members of the rap group Grandmaster Flash and the Furious Five, a Japanese newspaper reporter who happily gave up her press-box seat to sit with the real fans, and an elderly cowbell-wielding man named Ali, who commuted from his native Puerto Rico every baseball season to watch his team in action.

But being a Yankee fan also meant weathering New York Yankees owner George Steinbrenner's recurrent threats to move the team to the swamplands of neighboring New Jersey. Yankee games became poignant with the fear that this could be the last generation to share in this sudden camaraderie. Meanwhile the city, pleading poverty, doubled the subway fare, while Steinbrenner, pleading poverty, redoubled his threats while quadrupling bleacher ticket prices. But it wasn't until a new mayor slashed social services to the bone while endorsing Steinbrenner's demand for a new midtown sports palace that the full extent of the story became clear: What was it about sports teams that they could find public money where the public couldn't?

Like other sports fans of long standing, we had worried over the yearly ritual of watching our teams declare their intentions to move to another city unless bribed with a new stadium or a new lease. As journalists concerned with urban issues, we wondered about the wisdom of city governments spending millions of dollars on these stadiums at a time when public housing, libraries, and schools were being dismantled at an unprecedented pace. Perhaps, we thought, there was a story in that.

What we found was more than a mere story. For one thing, the scale of the public subsidy was not millions of dollars, as we had thought, but *billions*—an expected $11 billion over the course of the 1990s, with no signs of slowing down.

We also discovered that the popular notion of the villains and the heroes in the battle over sports franchise blackmail was upside-down. Although newspapers had portrayed the public as unthinking fans who demanded their elected officials keep teams in town at any cost, we instead found hundreds of citizen activists who had been fighting city by city for years to stop public money from going to private profit. Corporate welfare, they called it, and understandably so. Meanwhile, the local politicians who had pleaded that they had no choice but to give in to sports owners' demands turned out to be eagerly lining up to build sparkling new luxury boxes—where they then happily attended games as the owners' special guests. As one fed-up city resident told us, "They're not public servants. They're corporate servants."

This book began because we were frustrated with free-agent franchises demanding money as the price of their loyalty. But this is far more than a sports story: It's also a story of deceptive politicians, taxpayer swindles, media slants, the power of big money, and most of all, a political system that serves the rich and powerful at the expense of the average fan, the average taxpayer, the average citizen.

The more we learned in researching this book, the more apparent it became that the most important partner in the new stadium tango has been left out for far too long. Average citizens are the ones paying for the cost of new sports facilities—in public subsidies, in tax revenue lost, in public spaces taken over for private gain, in disillusionment with the democratic process, and in the loss of sheer enjoyment at being a spectator at a pro sporting event. We spoke with heartbroken sports fans who couldn't imagine life without their team, and neighborhood activists just struggling to make ends meet. One outraged citizen, questioning the whole concept of public money going to sports facilities, wondered aloud if his love of bowling meant he should get state money to build new bowling lanes. Another has vowed never to patronize the monolithic stadium his once-beloved home team is about to build. All were willing to open their memories, their homes, and their lives to our inquiries and curiosity.

We remain overwhelmed and moved by the stories these people had to share. Yes, this is the tale of the Art Modells and George Steinbrenners of the world, but more than anything it is the average citizen's story: the story of people across the country saying "enough is enough" with corporate welfare in all its many forms.

We ultimately tracked the roots of the sports stadium swindle back in time to the construction of the railroads in 19th-century America, and into the corridors of local power politics in a hundred towns across the United States and Canada. But the story of the swindle really begins on the night it first broke through to public consciousness: a cold spring night in a Maryland suburb, when a fleet of moving vans crept away in

the dead of night—stealing a city's football team away, and forever changing the way we think about sports, urban politics,
and the future of the American city.

1 A TALE OF TWO INNER CITIES

> *"It is simply unconscionable that cities are forced to succumb to blackmail by pro football and baseball. You should not capitulate to blackmailers. You don't deal with hostage situations. You don't deal with terrorists. I put these teams in the same category."*
> —MARYLAND STATE SENATOR JULIAN LAPIDES[1]

It was late in the night of March 29, 1984, when a dozen moving vans backed up to the football training complex in the Maryland suburb of Owings Mills and took the Baltimore Colts away.

Since 1953 the Colts had been an institution as fundamental to Baltimore's self-image as crabcakes or Edgar Allan Poe. Now, overnight, this symbol of the city was to be reborn as something called the Indianapolis Colts, and disappear forever into an indoor football stadium in the American heartland.

A few spectators gathered in the rain to watch as the worldly belongings of Baltimore's football team were loaded up for the 600-mile drive west. The movers, imported from Indianapolis' Mayflower van lines by Colts owner Robert Irsay for the occasion, packed away helmets and pads, file cabinets and film projectors, as Pinkerton guards kept onlookers at bay.

"It's unbelievable, the callousness of this man," Colts fan Brian Yaniger told a crowd of assembled reporters. "Just because he has a couple of bucks, he can tear a whole city down on his whims."[2]

The Colts' move was hardly the first time a pro sports team switched cities. In 1958, after all, the Dodgers had famously fled Brooklyn, and six of the National Basketball Association's inaugural eight teams had moved from their original homes by 1963. The first great era of sports franchise migration ran from 1952 until 1968—when the Kansas City (née Philadelphia) A's ended their two-decade westward flight by settling in Oakland. In the interim, more than a dozen sports franchises took up new residences.

But those were different times. Jet travel had abruptly made bicoastal leagues a reality, and the great population shifts away from the urban centers of the Northeast to the suburbs and the Sunbelt had opened up new markets for pro sports. By the time the Colts took flight, the major sports leagues had already expanded into most of the attractive locations, and franchise shifts had become rare. Before the Oakland Raiders moved to Los Angeles in 1982, no established football team had switched cities in two decades. Baseball hadn't seen a move in 12 years; basketball and hockey had undergone unprecedented expansion but little franchise movement since the early '70s. Sports fans in Baltimore, like their counterparts across the nation, had grown secure in the expectation that their team would still be there to cheer on the following year.

Besides, the team's absentee owner, Robert Irsay, had just been handed $25 million in city-funded stadium improvements to quiet earlier threats to leave town. And the team was moving to Indianapolis of all places, a city no larger than Baltimore, with only a single major-league team to its name, the fledgling Indiana Pacers basketball club—a prototypical hick town derisively nicknamed India-no-place.

The Colts' move, clearly, was something new and frightening: a team leaving its home of three decades not for lack of support (the Colts had continued to attract large crowds in its last years in Baltimore), but solely for the lure of greater profits. "If the Colts can be moved that way," wrote *New York Times* sports columnist Dave Anderson following the team's midnight flight, "any other franchise area in any sport can wake up some morning to find itself without a team."[3]

They were prophetic words. The Colts' move may have seemed an anomaly at the time, but in retrospect it was the dawn of an era. In 1984, corporations large and small were learning as never before how to supplement profits by extorting money from their hometowns under threat of moving across the country or overseas. The sports industry may have come late to this game of "corporate welfare," as it came to be known, but it soon had adopted the tactic for its own. While a manufacturing plant could win perhaps tens of millions of dollars this way, the final tab for a single sports subsidy could run as high as half a billion dollars.

The Colts' sudden move led to a series of events far beyond anything that could have been imagined that spring night. By the time the dust had settled, another football team had been taken from its diehard fans, and two cities had undertaken the building of four new stadiums, leaving taxpayers in two states to pay close to $1 billion in construction costs. The resulting transfer of public funds into private pockets would lay claim to public schools and fragile urban neighborhoods, leave democratic checks and balances in shambles, and enrich a handful of owners—real estate barons and wealthy industrialists—by hundreds of millions of dollars. The flight of the Baltimore Colts may have seemed like the end of the world for the team's fans, but for sports owners, it was the beginning of a lucrative dream that has yet to end. Before long, Cleveland, another urban center similarly struggling to survive the shifting industrial landscape of the 1970s, would be drawn into the musical-chairs game of relocating sports teams and earmarking public funds for stadium construction. Within a decade, nearly every major city in the nation was being asked to mortgage its future to the sports industry, and Robert Irsay was beginning to look less like a singular demon than the harbinger of a scam of historic proportions.

It all started, inauspiciously enough, with the Hoosier Dome.

Take the Money and Run

The idea was first floated in the mid-1970s by business and political leaders in Indianapolis. The local government had already poured more than $400 million into a decade's worth of downtown office blocks and hotel complexes; a new domed football stadium, they proposed, would complement the city's convention center as the centerpiece of a hub of sports-based tourism.[4] Construction of the Hoosier Dome was under way by 1982, its $78 million price tag financed by a one percent countywide tax on food and beverages and $30 million in grants from two local foundations.[5]

Indianapolis had a state-of-the-art domed stadium rising in its city center, but it still had no team. Dome boosters had assured city leaders that the NFL would place an expansion football team in Indianapolis once construction was complete. By 1982, however, it had become clear that the football league was in no hurry to expand—thanks in part to an ongoing lawsuit over the Raiders' move to Los Angeles the previous year.[6] Furthermore, it was looking more likely that, once expansion did arrive, the NFL would favor booming Sunbelt cities such as Phoenix and Jacksonville over Indianapolis. Articles started appearing in financial publications with such headlines as "Will Indianapolis' Domed Stadium Become a White Elephant?"[7]

This, clearly, would not do. So three-term mayor William Hudnut, sensing political disaster, reestablished an old contact he had made back in 1977, when the dome was still just a set of blueprints: He called Robert Irsay, owner of the Baltimore Colts. And he offered him a deal.

A Chicago industrialist who had made his fortune in sheet metal, Irsay had bought the Colts in 1972 and watched as his new team took an immediate nosedive in the standings. In 1979, with the Colts floundering on the field and in ticket sales, the team's owner demanded that the city pay for $25 million worth of improvements to 25-year-old Memorial Stadium, which the Colts shared with the Baltimore Orioles baseball team. If not, he intimated, he would take his team elsewhere.[8]

The city capitulated to the Colts' owner's demands, but still Irsay's eye wandered. By 1984, his flirtations had focused on Indianapolis, where Hudnut was offering a low-rent lease on the new dome to entice the team to relocate. Baltimore city officials, scrambling to keep the Colts in place, countered with an offer of a $15 million loan and a city-backed guarantee on ticket sales. But even as they held out this lucrative carrot to Irsay, city leaders also readied an unprecedented stick: They asked the state legislature to consider condemning the team via the principle of eminent domain.

Under eminent domain powers, local governments can condemn a private asset and then seize it, paying the former owners fair market value for their property—in this case, the Colts themselves, which would then be sold to a new, local owner. It's a tactic more often used for highway rights-of-way than for football teams; it's also one that had failed two years earlier in Oakland when the Raiders skipped town. But that case had been rejected by an appeals court on very narrow grounds, and legal experts were hopeful that the city of Baltimore would have better luck with its case.

It never got the chance. The Colts, tipped off to the city's plans, hurriedly completed negotiations with Indianapolis.[9] And so, on March 29, 1984, while the Maryland legislature continued to debate the use of eminent domain, in came the moving vans. That afternoon, the bill to place the Colts under state control was passed, but it was a few hours too late: Courts would later rule against the seizure on the grounds that by the time the law was passed, there was nothing left for the state to seize.

The Baltimore Colts were no more. As fans grieved, local politicians plotted to obtain a replacement franchise, either through expansion or by moving an established team. And city officials across the nation braced for a new wave of demands from their own sports teams, under threat of becoming "another Baltimore."

"Mistake on the Lake"

The last thing the city of Cleveland wanted was to become the next Baltimore. It was already the first, and hopefully last, Cleveland, and that was enough of an emotional burden for even the windy town's hardiest souls. Once a thriving industrial center with dominating sports teams, Cleveland had seen its fortunes, its national image, and the reputation of its historic baseball stadium plummet over mere decades.

In 1931, the successful completion of the new sports stadium on the shores of Lake Erie was hailed as the harbinger of great things to come. Cleveland Municipal Stadium, built by the federal Works Project Administration with the hope of luring the 1932 Olympics to downtown Cleveland, was "a monument to the progressive spirit of the city's people," according to the special section of the Cleveland *Plain Dealer* devoted to the new stadium.[10]

The city, not yet crippled under the weight of the Depression, was coming off one of its most successful economic decades ever. Cleveland had become the nation's second largest center for automobile manufacturing, behind only Detroit. Big steel was thriving, as was manufacturing. And the brand-new horseshoe by the lake, built at a cost of some $2.5 million to local taxpayers, was the crown jewel in an economic construction plan designed to give the city even more national attention. When 80,000 fans jammed into Municipal Stadium's wooden seats for the Cleveland Indians' first baseball game there in 1932, headline writers crowed "Depression Given Black Eye."[11] It was there that the team reveled in its glory years of the 1940s and 1950s, when the Indians were one of the most successful teams in baseball and their fans set attendance records that would last for decades.

Fifty years later, the stadium had assumed a very different meaning. Municipal Stadium, and the city itself, became dubbed the "Mistake on the Lake." As Cleveland struggled through a series of national embarrassments in the 1970s— from the Cuyahoga River catching on fire to becoming the first major American city to go into default since the Depression—the dreadful performance of the Indians, and their aging ballpark, seemed horribly symbolic of Cleveland's misfortunes. Year after cellar-dwelling year, the team was considered an embarrassment to professional baseball, and talk escalated that opposing teams dreaded the trip to frigid Cleveland Municipal Stadium, with its bitter winds off Lake Erie and its tiny crowds, cramped locker rooms, and out-of-date scoreboard.[12]

And while many in the city turned critical eyes on the performance of the Indians, Cleveland itself was feeling the uncomfortable burn of a national spotlight that illuminated a shrinking population, deteriorating race relations, escalating poverty, and vanishing industrial jobs. The city, which had lost 23 percent of its population between 1970 and 1980, started the 1980s with its credit suspended by several Wall Street ratings agencies because of its fiscal woes.[13]

When Indians owner Steve O'Neill died in 1983, rumors ran rampant that the financially shaky team would be sold to buyers from another state, most likely Florida. Even before O'Neill's death, league officials had come to town to announce that the Indians were very likely not long for Cleveland. Without a principal owner for the team, its future was suddenly even more precarious. And so in 1984 a new tax initiative to fund a domed stadium (domes were then in fashion, as several cities had followed Indianapolis' lead) was called for, in order, it was claimed, to keep the team in the city.

The campaign for the dome was the brainchild of Cuyahoga County Commissioner Vincent Campanella. Working largely without the organized support of his fellow politicians, Campanella proposed putting a domed stadium in the old Central Market area of downtown Cleveland; the new $150 million, 72,000-seat stadium was to be entirely paid for by a countywide property tax levy.

Emotions ran high among fans and residents throughout the dome debate. The way some locals talked, the threatened move of a sports team would tear the heart out of the city. Yet many Clevelanders questioned the fiscal sanity of forking over public dollars at a time when the town overall was struggling to reverse years of financial woe. Others were reluctant to spend a great deal of tax money on a team that had performed so abysmally for so many years. "Go Browns," a cynical graffitist scrawled on the walk to Municipal Stadium. "And take the Indians with you."

In May 1984, voters resoundingly rejected the proposal. The choice of a property tax to fund the initiative, the poor performance by the Indians on the playing field, and, most important, a lack of consensus among the city's power brokers probably sent the campaign to its defeat.[14] The effort never had the full support of then-Governor Richard Celeste or the city's Republican mayor, George Voinovich. Indeed, Campanella himself would later speculate that the failure of the domed stadium tax killed his political career.[15]

But if Campanella's mishandling of the political situation temporarily doomed the dome, the *idea* of a new stadium had plenty of support, especially from the city's powerful business community. As would become the national pattern, advertisements by dome supporters promised Cleveland taxpayers that the new stadium would result in magnificent economic dividends for the city as a whole, promises that continued after the referendum went down to a solid defeat. Soon after the initiative lost, *The Washington Post* reported, "Cleveland leaders can't ignore a study that said a dome would result in the construction of three new downtown hotels, an office building and restaurants, that 1,588 full-time construction jobs would be created; that another 6,829 permanent jobs would result; that the total annual spending impact would be $62.2 million."[16] National and local media, the business community and local politicians all firmly pushed the idea that a new stadium was needed for the team and for Cleveland's hopes of re-establishing itself as an important city.

And although their referendum failed, domed stadium backers didn't give up. The Civic Committee to Build a Domed Stadium was formed, chaired by the acting chair of the Greater Cleveland Growth Association, the town's chamber of commerce.[17] The Civic Committee would later become the Greater Cleveland Domed Stadium Corporation, which borrowed $22 million from local banks and the state in order to purchase a site for a new facility.[18] Despite public opposition and construction and financing plans that were sketchy at best, supporters were determined to plunge ahead with the stadium project.

Before Cleveland's power brokers could come up with a new pitch, however, the national sports stadium scene irrevocably shifted—thanks in large part to events taking place back in Baltimore.

"Just Give Me the Tools"
The departure of the Colts in the spring of 1984 had an immediate impact on Baltimore politics. Seeing the outcry over the loss of one sports team, Mayor William Schaefer, who had

been a steadfast opponent of spending public money on sports stadiums, abruptly became the biggest booster of a new ballpark for the Baltimore Orioles.

A success on the field and off since relocating from St. Louis in 1954, the Baltimore club ran off seven first-place finishes between 1966 and 1979, and their home at city-owned Memorial Stadium was a pleasant one, nestled in a residential neighborhood of single-family homes whose rooftops were visible beyond the wooden bleachers in right and left fields. In the mid-1980s, a poll of fans ranked Memorial as one of the best ballparks in the major leagues.

But for all its pastoral charm, Memorial was a no-frills ballpark, without such modern-day amenities as luxury boxes or lavish food preparation facilities. As early as 1967, when municipalities across the country were building new concrete "dual-purpose" stadiums to house both their football and baseball teams, the owners of the Colts and Orioles had proposed such a facility for Baltimore, to be situated near the old Camden railyards just west of downtown. In 1972, Orioles exec Frank Cashen upped the ante, proclaiming, "We are not going to be able to do anything in terms of a new long-term lease unless a stadium is built downtown."[19] But as it became clear that no such deal was forthcoming, the Orioles continued to sign short-term leases on Memorial, and no one moved to resurrect the idea of a new facility.

Then, in 1979, local beer magnate Jerrold Hoffberger sold the Orioles to Edward Bennett Williams, a lawyer-to-the-pols from hated rival Washington, D.C. Many in Baltimore suspected Williams of harboring secret plans to move the ballclub to the nation's capital—a suspicion that the new owner wasted no time in using to force the city's hand on his demands for a new stadium. "For as long as the city will support the team," he told The Washington Post, "it will stay here"—leading to rampant speculation that he would take the team south on the pretext of low attendance.[20] When American League President Lee MacPhail followed with a public vow of league support for a new stadium on I-95 between Baltimore and Washington, the pressure built for Baltimore to prevent a repeat of the Colts' betrayal.

By 1986, when Mayor Schaefer was elected governor of Maryland, he was not just a proponent of a new baseball stadium; he had become Williams' greatest ally. The man who as mayor had declared that "unless private enterprise builds it, we won't build it" was now missing no opportunity to stump for a new state-built ballpark.[21] Bill Marker, a local community leader who would play a major role in the stadium battle to come, recalls watching Schaefer's inaugural speech as governor: "I remember saying to friends, 'Well, let's see whether he mentions the stadium, and if so where in his speech.' And it was basically: 'Hi, Marylanders! We've gotta build a stadium!'"

Schaefer knew just where he wanted to build it, too: the same Camden Yards site that had been considered for a multisport facility back in the '60s. Ten years earlier, Mayor Schaefer had helped mastermind the reconstruction of Baltimore's inner harbor as the Harborplace mall-and-museum tourist mecca. Now, Governor Schaefer concluded that a stadium could only enhance the attractiveness of the city's rebuilt downtown to out-of-towners and their entertainment dollars.

To keep Williams happy, Schaefer was prepared to build the project entirely with public money, proposing two state-run lotteries with a sports theme to raise the $235 million necessary to condemn the existing industrial park on the site and to fund the construction of separate stadiums for baseball and football. (As it turned out, Schaefer had seriously underestimated the cost of clearing land for the project. The total tab would ultimately reach $410 million, plus an additional $30 million for road improvements, to be paid out of federal transportation funds.)

The plan was cemented at a memorable public hearing of
the state senate in March 1987. The star attraction was
Williams, who used every bit of his personal charm and political connections to sway the legislators. In attendance that day
was Bill Marker, preparing to testify on behalf of his fledgling
Marylanders for Sports Sanity (MASS), a hastily organized citizens' group opposing public stadium funding. His hand-drawn
placards, detailing alternate proposals that MASS had calcu-
lated could keep the team in town for far less money—including having the state buy the team outright for less than the
cost of a new stadium—sat unused at his feet as he watched
Williams testify at length that a new ballpark was the only
solution to the woes of his team, as well as those of Baltimore.
The governor, recalls Marker, was greeted as an old friend: "It
was all these senators saying, 'Oh, you were my professor in law
school, and you were so wonderful.'"

While Marker sat, several legislators expressed concerns
about spending such a large sum on what was, after all, a private enterprise. When Williams remarked that he needed a
stadium that could guarantee sales of 15,000 season tickets,
state senator Julian "Jack" Lapides shot back, "It might be
cheaper for the state to buy fifteen thousand season tickets."
Williams waited for the cheers from the gallery to die down,
then replied, "I didn't come here to ask for a subsidy....I can
make this thing go in the private sector if I get the tools."[22]

The "tools" Williams wanted—a taxpayer-funded stadium—represented just as much of a subsidy as a direct cash
grant, of course, but the state senate didn't let that stand in its
way. Four weeks after Williams' testimony, the senate voted to
empower the Maryland Sports Authority to build two new
stadiums: a baseball park immediately for the Orioles, and a
football stadium to follow once a replacement for the Colts
could be lined up.

With the governor, state legislature, and mayor united behind a publicly funded ballpark, Marker and his fellow community activists had only one weapon left at their disposal. According to the Maryland state constitution, any government expenditure can be submitted to a binding public referendum. Within two weeks of the state senate decision, MASS had gone door-to-door to gather 28,000 signatures calling for a public vote. The state rejected the petitions on the grounds that the stadium funding bill was not subject to referendum; MASS took the state to court. An initial ruling sided with the neighborhood activists. But that September, the Maryland court of appeals overturned the lower court's ruling, agreeing with the state's argument that the stadium project constituted an "appropriation for maintaining the state government" and so was exempt from public vote.

"I think they lost the distinction that the state was doing it for a private enterprise," Jack Lapides now says of the court's ruling. "If the state were condemning the land, and building the facility for a *state* football team, or a state road, or a state hospital, or a state school, then there would be justification. But I thought that their rationale was very convoluted."

Opponents screamed long and loud that Schaefer had bullied his way past the democratic process, but the deed was done. The stadium—given the cumbersome appellation "Oriole Park at Camden Yards" at the insistence of Eli Jacobs, who bought the Orioles following Williams' death in 1988—had cleared its final hurdle. On April 6, 1992, five years and $120 million worth of lottery tickets later, the new ballpark opened to a packed house. And the value of Jacobs' team, according to figures compiled by *Financial World* magazine, jumped by nearly $100 million.

At long last, the new stadium had taken its place alongside the other government-sponsored tourist attractions that now crowded the city's Inner Harbor. But as important as it was to

Baltimore, Oriole Park at Camden Yards was destined to play a still more pivotal role in the history of pro sports. For the Orioles had insisted on a building that would be not an antiseptic stadium but an intimate *ballpark*; unlike every other baseball stadium built in recent memory, this one eschewed concrete walls and symmetrical dimensions for a self-consciously quirky design that used steel and brick to sheath its luxury boxes and ad-filled video screens. From the upper-deck seats, fans were treated to vistas not of suburban parking lots but of the city skyline. In a final touch that delighted architectural critics and baseball fans alike, the right-field wall abutted an 87-year-old brick warehouse that was converted into team offices, a baseball museum, and upscale shops.[23]

As Camden Yards biographer Peter Richmond wrote, "Baltimore didn't need a new baseball stadium, but it was more than grateful for the deliverance of a national showpiece."[24] Camden Yards, as the park would soon be known nationwide, caught the attention of every baseball team yearning for a new stadium. As fans flocked through the gates of the new "old-time" park, filling the Orioles' ledgers with unprecedented revenue, the repercussions would be felt nationwide.

"Comeback City"

While the Orioles' new owner was lobbying for a new home in Baltimore, the hapless Indians (helmless as well after O'Neill's death) were about to see their fortunes change. Whether real or imagined, the threat of losing its baseball franchise, no matter how much the Indians had struggled, was of enormous importance to many Clevelanders. The city had witnessed, as had the rest of the country, what had happened to Baltimore's beloved Colts when another town laid down better terms. So when, two years after the domed stadium went down in defeat at the polls, the Indians were bought by Richard and David Jacobs, there was a collective sigh of relief. The Jacobses (no relation to Orioles owner Eli Jacobs) were local brothers who had made millions in real estate development, especially in shopping mall constructions. Significantly, they had made their fortunes in the Cleveland area and had considerable interest in downtown development projects.[25] "Increasingly they began to make substantial investments in the city of Cleveland," explains David R. Elkins, a professor of political science at Cleveland State University, noting that the brothers purchased building after building in the downtown area. "They made some enormous changes on the physical appearance of the city."

There wouldn't be much of a grace period for Clevelanders, however, because the Jacobs brothers weren't about to give up on the idea of having a new home built for their team. The brothers had made their fortunes in an industry that had benefited tremendously for decades from Cleveland's generous tax abatement policies, and when they bought the Indians, they argued that a central element to their successful rebuilding of the team would have to be a new home. But in a city that had already rejected public funding of a new stadium, it would take masterful manipulation to persuade the populace to fund such a project.

In 1990, the Central Market Gateway Project was formed in order to develop a new downtown stadium for the Indians and arena for the basketball Cavaliers (who had been playing in suburban Richfield) with what was then proposed as a mix of public and private funds. The project got its title from the proposed construction site—28 acres of prime downtown real estate that was home to the city's historic Central Market. The site was one of the city's two old open-air produce and supply markets and was still an active, if somewhat neglected, neighborhood gathering spot when it was demolished in 1989 at the request of the domed stadium supporters. For several years, as stadium backers plotted tactics, the site sat, unused, as Cleveland's inner-city residents were forced to go elsewhere for their shopping needs. Those same taxpayers presumably could take solace, along with the rest of the city, in thinking of the newly razed spot as the centerpiece for what had been dubbed a "comeback city."

With property taxes a proven failure with voters and politicians alike, the principal means of paying off the city bonds that would fund the new stadium project was to be a "sin tax"—a tax on alcoholic beverages and cigarette- and tobacco-related products. The Cuyahoga County commissioners, no doubt fearful of tying their own political futures to such a project, decided to put that decision to the voters—against the wishes of stadium boosters, who desperately wanted to have the county impose the tax without a costly referendum campaign. Raising $1 million from private interests, including $300,000 from both the Indians and the Cavaliers, supporters of the initiative set out to prove to Cleveland voters that a vote for the stadium was a vote for the future of Cleveland.[26]

"Who wins with Issue 2?" blared a newspaper ad just days before the 1990 vote. "We All Do," answered the placards held by a multicultural rainbow of Cleveland schoolchildren. "Gateway will create a development that will generate $33.7 million in public revenues every year and provide: 28,000 good-paying jobs for the *jobless*; Neighborhood housing development for the *homeless*; $15 million a year for schools for our *children*; revenues for City and County clinics and hospitals for the *sick*; energy assistance programs for the *elderly*." The ad went on to promise what wouldn't be taken from taxpayers' wallets or given to team owners: "No property tax; no sales tax; no income tax; no tax abatement…Gateway: the next chapter in our future."[27]

The PR campaign was combined with some hardball threats from the Major League Baseball establishment. Two days before the vote, baseball commissioner Fay Vincent paid a visit to the city of Cleveland. "Should this facility not be available in Cleveland, should the vote be a negative one, we may be finding ourselves confronting a subject that we want to avoid," Vincent said. "I say to you, it would be very bad for baseball, and I am opposed to Cleveland losing its team."[28] A *Plain Dealer* columnist laid it out for the public: "Anyone who thinks the Indians will still be playing in [Municipal] Stadium at the end of the century is nuts. They'll either be in a new stadium here or a new stadium elsewhere. Period."[29]

The so-called Gateway initiative won a narrow victory with 51.7 percent of the vote.[30] As with the earlier domed stadium initiative, all but one of the 21 wards located within the city limits voted against the proposal.

The voting reflected a split in the local electorate, explains John Ryan, executive secretary of the Cleveland AFL-CIO. "One is the suburbanites and a couple of wards that have quite a bit of money. The other are low-income people or people that rely on the school systems. And for the most part they are people who don't have much of a voice." The stadium vote had reaffirmed working-class and poor Clevelanders' suspicions that, when it came to matters of public policy and decision-making in the city, their pocketbooks were the first to be raided (via cigarette and liquor taxes, which, like all taxes on the sale of goods, fall disproportionately on those with lower incomes), even though their concerns were the last to be addressed.

Voters had approved the proposal with the understanding that the combined cost of the new stadium and arena would run about $343 million. But that soon turned into a much greater public investment—some estimate the total cost through 1996 to be as high as $462 million, with as much as two-thirds coming from the public. And that cost is still accumulating.[31] It wasn't until late December 1996 that the Gateway Economic Development Corp. signed a contract agreeing to pay, over five years, $1.6 million in overdue taxes—most of it owed to Cleveland schools.[32]

"The arena was the real bugaboo," says Elkins. The Cavaliers played in a nearly new arena in nearby Richfield, he explains, and the team owners, Gordon and George Gund, had just refurbished that arena at their own expense. The Gunds, he recalls, "were constantly saying, 'We don't need to come downtown. We have a fine facility out at Richfield Coliseum, and if we don't have a state-of-the-art facility here in Cleveland, there's no incentive, more or less, for us to come downtown.'"

Cost overruns or not, by the spring of 1994 the Indians had their new home. (Gund Arena, for the Cavaliers, would follow the next year.) Named Jacobs Field after Richard Jacobs offered the highest bid for the naming rights, the new stadium was directly in the Camden Yards mold—intimately sized, constructed out of lime rock to reflect local construction resources, with an asymmetrical seat layout and state-of-the-art scoreboard.

Send in the Browns

Even while some Clevelanders bemoaned a stadium seen as too big, too old, and too drafty for baseball, the town's football team continued to pack in crowds at the same location. The Cleveland Browns, owned since 1961 by multimillionaire GOP fundraiser Art Modell, were as much a symbol of NFL glory as the Indians were a baseball embarrassment. All winter long, Sunday afternoons meant packed Browns games at Municipal Stadium with a boisterous core of working-class fans who'd cheered the team on for decades. The rabid enthusiasm was symbolized by the nationally known "Dawg Pound"—the rowdy crowd of fans in the endzone bleacher seats who painted themselves in the team's orange and brown, often consumed great quantities of alcohol, and usually donned canine masks when the team's defensive secondary took to calling themselves the Dawgs and barking. (Arsenio Hall would immortalize this group by encouraging his late-night national television audience to bark in the same manner.)

By the mid-1980s, when the fate of the Indians was portrayed as being in severe jeopardy, the future of the Browns was never publicly questioned.[33] But on November 4, 1995, Modell stunned the city with the revelation that he had been involved in negotiations with Maryland officials to move his team to Baltimore. Rumors had circulated for months that Modell resented the city finding money to build the Gateway Project and the new Rock and Roll Hall of Fame while not funding renovations of Municipal Stadium. But Modell had also promised the city in 1994 that as long as he owned the team he'd never leave town, and the rumors remained just that—until November 1995.[34]

Modell had long requested renovations to Municipal Stadium, and some were in the works. In fact, the story of his probable exodus broke the day before a scheduled vote to extend the sin tax created to fund the Gateway complex so that it could be used to pay for improvements to the Browns' home. Perhaps not surprisingly (*The Plain Dealer* ran a front-page editorial urging a yes vote), the referendum passed.

But with a lucrative offer from Baltimore in hand, Modell was not about to be placated with stadium renovations. Three days later, the deal was official. Cries of fury came from almost every corner of Cleveland. From carefully orchestrated petition drives by the mayor's office, to spontaneous anti-Modell outbursts (at times lapsing into anti-Semitism—"They killed the wrong Jew" read one memorable homemade sign at a Browns game after Israeli Prime Minister Yitzhak Rabin was slain), the city reacted with passion and outrage to Modell's announcement.

There were several "Save Our Browns" rallies in the months following Modell's announcement—especially after Mayor Michael White urged Clevelanders to let the nation hear their outrage. "No Team, No Peace" was a common slogan in a surreal time in which a city saw its usually moderate mayor tirelessly campaign against one of the town's most famous multimillion-dollar residents. Concerned citizens wore orange armbands and gathered petitions, Cleveland-born comedian Drew Carey spoke at one rally, and a cottage industry blossomed of anti-Modell T-shirts, buttons, and bumper stickers. But the Browns left anyway, and the city reeled. It was perhaps the only time *The New York Times* has ever run a photograph of a grown man wearing a dog mask, smoking a cigar, and weeping.[35]

As for Baltimore, after 12 years the city finally had found its replacement for the Colts, even if the new Baltimore Ravens didn't yet have quite the allure of the old club. The Browns' move also meant that Baltimore would at last have to build the new stadium that it had denied the Colts, a football-only stadium adjacent to Oriole Park at Camden Yards, at a cost of an additional $200 million in state lottery money. For the Ravens, there was no question of paying their own way: Their new lease guaranteed the team 30 years of free rent, plus a $50 million cash relocation bonus. "As sweetheart [deals] go, call this one the Demi Moore special," *San Diego Union-Tribune* sportswriter Tom Cushman wrote, noting that a Ravens subsidiary would even rake in half the profits (plus a ten percent "management fee") for rock concerts and other non-football events at the new stadium.[36] The Orioles, noting a parity clause in their lease requiring that they get at least a good a deal as any football team at Camden Yards, immediately demanded free rent, too.

Baltimore had paid dearly to replace its departed football team; now it would be Cleveland's turn to ante up. The city had hoped that the renovation of Municipal Stadium voters had approved in November would be enough to lure a new team. But when Mayor White met with NFL officials in early January 1996, he was told that the league would only consider a replacement team if there was a new stadium in place.[37] White, following negotiations with NFL officials on the city's chances of getting a replacement football team, quickly brokered a deal to tear down Municipal Stadium and replace it with a new $220 million football-only stadium to be paid for primarily with tax money.[38]

A populace that had just been called upon to hand over $175 million in stadium renovation money was now going to have its wallets raided once again. And yet, with the very real specter of a town without football facing Cleveland voters and politicians, local activists calling for a change in fiscal priorities faced an uphill battle.

Marge Misak, a longtime community activist, remembers well her sense of isolation. "There was no outcry. There were no people publicly, no politicians, no groups, that were saying, 'Wait a minute. Let's look at it. Let's question it.' It was astounding, especially in light of the fact that all the cost overruns at Gateway were coming through, and the county was coming up with more and more loans that were obviously not going to be repaid, just to finish that project….It was kind of an astounding juxtaposition, because you would think that there would be questions about, 'Did we learn our lesson here?'"

Six days of debate in the Cleveland City Council culminated in a 13-8 vote in support of funding the new football stadium. The final tally was closer than many had expected. At the council hearings, recalls Misak, "One councilperson got up and talked about his neighborhood and the children, apologizing to the eight-year-olds in his neighborhood who didn't have swings to play on. In the beginning of his speech I thought, 'Oh my gosh. I can't believe this person, who is a total mayor's ally.' I'm thinking he's going to come out against this…." She trails off in a laugh. "But he didn't! He apologized to all the eight-year-olds in his neighborhood and then voted to put the city general fund at risk."

By February 1996, *The Plain Dealer* could boast in its lead editorial, "The best deal possible; Cleveland is rid of Art Modell and his mediocre team, and Mayor White has helped foster a Browns rebirth."[39] It was civic-boostering spin at an all-time peak—what had been painted as tragedy only a few short months before was now seen as the only possible way for the city to hold on to its team name and rid itself of a suddenly unpopular man at the same time. No one dared mention that the city coffers didn't have the money to fund a new stadium— Cleveland's third publicly funded new sports facility in less than a decade—or that acquiring a new team could very well mean enticing a team to bolt from yet another town.

Early reports had the Cincinnati Bengals or, ironically enough, the Indianapolis Colts being brought in to play in the new Cleveland stadium. But the Bengals soon took themselves out of the running by striking a deal for their own new stadium—paid for lock, stock, and luxury box by the citizens of Cincinnati to keep their football team in town. The March 1996 referendum that authorized that football stadium also approved a new stadium for the baseball Reds to keep them from feeling left out. And so, by the spring of 1997, plans had been laid for four stadiums in two states as a consequence of Art Modell's flight from Cleveland, itself a product of the Colts' move from Baltimore over a decade before.

Aftermath

According to today's conventional media wisdom, both Cleveland and Baltimore are cities in the midst of "renaissances," rising from the ashes of '70s decay to stand newly triumphant as urban growth centers. Credit for these rebirths is largely given to the cities' reconstructed downtowns, anchored in each case by a multimillion-dollar sports complex that draws tourists from across the country.

Indeed, it's hard to imagine how the new stadiums could be more successful. Jacobs Field and Camden Yards were virtual sellouts from the day they opened; in 1996 and 1997, the Indians set a new baseball record by selling out the *entire season* months before opening day, leaving the team's ticket sales staff with little to do for the year but count the money. A study by the city of Baltimore found that the number of fans coming into town from outside the Baltimore-Washington region for Orioles games nearly doubled after the new ballpark was built.

As for the visions of a rising economic tide that would lift all boats, though, the story was more troubling. And so while Cleveland, under the leadership of Mayor White, has been lauded repeatedly by the national media as a classic comeback town—with its beautiful new sports facilities as key ingredients—life remains much the same for the city's still shrinking urban population. In the midst of a decades-long drop in population, the percentage of Clevelanders living in poverty rose from 17 percent in 1970 to over 40 percent by the mid-1990s.[40] The city school system, drained of property taxes, is in shambles—only 38 percent of its students graduate high school, with only seven percent testing at a 12th-grade level—and was placed in state receivership in 1995.[41] In fact, the day before the deal for a new football stadium in Cleveland was approved by the Cleveland city council, the Cleveland public school system announced it would cut $52 million over two years, laying off up to 160 teachers and eliminating interscholastic athletics from a program that Cleveland School Superintendent Richard A. Boyd described as "in the worst financial shape of any school district in the country."[42]

In Baltimore, the toll is harder to quantify. Since the stadiums were built with state money, there is no guarantee that the city would have reaped the benefit of alternative uses for the funds. Still, the Camden Yards complex ultimately drew more than $400 million out of the state treasury, the bulk of it coming from poor Baltimoreans who are the lottery's best customers.[43] That's $400 million, critics charge, that could have been spent on the city's gaping chasm of needs for education or drug treatment. And the vein is now tapped out: With each new sports lottery to meet the stadiums' cost overruns, lottery state officials have seen their yield decline, leading many locals to conclude that the lottery market is simply saturated. In 1997, a plan to legalize limited casino gambling in the city of Baltimore and use the proceeds for education was shot down by Parris Glendening, Schaefer's successor as governor.

As for the neighborhood activists who had opposed Camden Yards, not all of their worst fears were realized. The surrounding neighborhoods, so far at least, have neither been gentrified beyond recognition nor lost in a flood of sports fan amenities. "They did a good job of doing a bad thing," concedes Bill Marker, looking up at the new stadium that literally casts a shadow over his mixed-income row-house neighborhood of Ridgely's Delight. True, the "historic" nature of the ballpark is more cosmetic than real; even the warehouse, without which the baseball field would, in Lapides' words, "just be sort of a blob sitting in the middle of a field," lost its northern end, lopped off to afford better views of the downtown skyline from the seats behind home plate. And the city did lose many of the 1,000 manufacturing jobs provided by the 26 companies that had existed on the Camden Yards site, as well as the property taxes that the food plants and other businesses had generated.[44]

Just across the highway from the new stadiums, the black enclave of Sharp-Leadenhall is less thrilled with its new neighbors, as it continues to plead for money from the city to repair its recreation center and swimming pool amid city cutbacks. "Oh man, the city," sighs Sharp-Leadenhall Planning Committee organizer May Ringold. "It's a pity that the city's there. We need some of that federal money. We're just a small community, but we've been around since the 17th century....If the stadium wanted to come into our neighborhood, I think they should try to help spruce up the neighborhood itself." The Stadium Authority's only offer to date: a new path through the community's playground, so that football fans could walk through more quickly on their way to the games.

Three miles to the north, in Baltimore's old sports center, the picture is more uniformly gloomy. Memorial Stadium now sits empty, save for the eight Sundays a year when the Ravens are in town, occupying the old bowl as they await their new digs at Camden Yards. The residential neighborhoods around the stadium, Waverly and Charles Village, whose modest brick houses provided the backdrop for so many Orioles and Colts games over the years, have started showing the first signs of decline: FOR SALE signs sprout like dandelions along 33rd Street and the shopping drag on nearby Greenmount Avenue is littered with empty storefronts. The Stadium Lounge, on Greenmount and 34th, bears two large signs in its window: "The Stadium Lounge Welcomes the NFL Baltimore Ravens" and "Checks Cashed in a Flash."

Jack Lapides, who is quick to praise the decision to place the new stadiums downtown instead of in the suburbs, is just as quick to point out that Baltimore already had a ballpark that met the same "old-time" criteria that would later draw compliments at Camden Yards. "The old Memorial Stadium was a perfectly valid ballpark," he says. "And it also would have kept up one of the few truly integrated neighborhoods in Baltimore, a nice middle-class neighborhood. People loved having the stadium there—many moved to the neighborhood because the stadium was there. And this was a nice draw in another part of the city, rather than putting everything in the Inner Harbor of Baltimore."

The greatest irony about these new sports palaces is that those who paid the most for them—the buyers of Maryland lottery tickets and Cleveland cigarettes—are the least able to enjoy them. Ticket pricing is steeper than in the old parks, though admittedly not quite as prohibitive as elsewhere in the country. But more important, the facilities often have fewer seats than their older counterparts, and that, coupled with a much greater number of luxury boxes and season tickets, has meant far fewer tickets available for the average fan.

Jacobs Field is beautiful, agrees union activist Ryan. "One of the things that happened though, I've noticed as a lifelong Indians fan, is that the increase in prices and the decrease in low ticket prices has made the crowd much more white. Incredibly much more white.

"And with the special parking and all that, the wealthier people don't mix with the working-class people for the most part. And to me that's disturbing. If you take a look at who's paying for that [with cigarette taxes], it is more the working-class people."

The cost of a game at Camden Yards is "prohibitive for a poor family," agrees Lapides. "You used to be able to go out to Memorial Stadium and sit in a fairly decent seat for three bucks. Three bucks won't even buy you a hot dog now at the new stadium."

If city schools and low-income fans were the losers in the twin stadium deals, the undeniable winners were the owners. The Orioles, bought by Eli Jacobs for $70 million while Camden Yards was still under construction in 1989, were resold in 1993 for $173 million, appreciating a whopping 147 percent in just four years.[45] Art Modell's football team jumped $38 million in value in one year when they left Cleveland for Baltimore. The Indians, whose new stadium coincided with the team's first contending team in 40 years, were the least-valued team in baseball in 1993, the year before Jacobs Field opened, with a value of $81 million; by 1996 the team had appreciated to $125 million, a tidy 54 percent profit in three years for the Jacobs brothers.[46]

Even if the increased attendance abates after the novelty of the new stadiums wears off, team owners can always hit up their hosts for a few renovations or lease improvements, under threat of once again taking their act on the road. "If it's not a personal toy of yours, if you are an owner and you have any fiduciary responsibility to anybody, and you *don't* demand a new facility, you're probably violating your fiduciary duty, given the way this stuff goes," notes Marker.

Fiduciary duty can rest easy. In the decade since the Colts' flight, not many owners would pass up the opportunity to levy demands on their city, or someone else's. Baltimore and Cleveland would prove to be merely the tip of the sports welfare iceberg.

2 STEALING HOME

"It's amazing what a pretty picture you can draw when you spend other people's money."
—HOUSTON RADIO STATION OWNER DAN PATRICK [1]

If it were only in Baltimore and Cleveland that the commotion over new stadiums reached such desperate extremes, it might be possible to write the two towns off as nothing more than a couple of sad coincidences—a pair of down-on-their-luck cities trying anything and everything to remake themselves. But in city after city, from Boston to Seattle, Los Angeles to Miami, Minneapolis to Houston, the story is the same: Team owners in the four biggest sports in the country—baseball, football, basketball, and hockey—are demanding new publicly funded stadiums and arenas and threatening to pull up and leave if they don't get them. North America is in the midst of a remarkable stadium and sports arena building boom unlike any other in its history. And municipalities large and small are paying the price for it—in massive public expenditures and tax abatements that lead to the loss of revenue for more worthy projects, and in the dismay and heartache of dedicated fans watching decades of loyalty and devotion trampled en route to the newest arena. Between 1980 and 1990, U.S. cities spent some $750 million on building or renovating sports arenas and stadiums. The bill for the '90s is expected to total anywhere between $8 billion and $11 billion, the bulk of it paid by taxpayers—and hidden subsidies could amount to billions more.[2]

By 1997, almost one-half of the country's 115 major professional sports franchises either were getting new or renovated facilities or had requested them. Indeed, in an era of increased public and government reluctance to lay out public money for anything—from food stamps to the local philharmonic—the eagerness with which cities are offering up hundreds of millions of dollars to build new stadiums is mind-boggling. Welfare as we know it may be dead, but corporate welfare is alive and kicking.

There are instances from sea to shining sea, encompassing every profit-making scheme imaginable. In San Francisco, the baseball Giants owners pushed four times for a publicly funded new stadium, and were four times rejected by Bay Area taxpayers—until winning a compromise on the fifth try. In south Florida, billionaire Wayne Huizenga is receiving a new home at taxpayer expense for his Florida Panthers hockey club after only four years of playing at Miami Arena. His co-tenants, the Miami Heat basketball team, will also soon move to a new facility down the coast, leaving the old arena vacant just ten years after it was built. Meanwhile, Denver built a $215 million baseball-only stadium with money from a sales tax hike in 1995 (for its new expansion franchise) and is now contemplating constructing a brand-new football stadium to placate an envious owner. The list includes towns like Seattle, where voters rejected a proposed tax hike to fund a new home for the Mariners but were ignored by a state legislature determined to see the new stadium funded at any cost, and Minneapolis, where Twins owners requested a replacement for a 15-year-old facility that the city is still paying off.

A new stadium didn't always mean massive amounts of public money—until the late 1940s and '50s, most professional sports teams played in privately owned facilities built by the teams' owners with their own revenues. But that changed in the ensuing decades; by the early 1990s, 77 percent of stadiums and arenas in use were publicly owned.[3] In the typical scenario, a municipality will float hundreds of millions of dollars in municipal bonds in order to afford the massive initial expenditure, and then pay off the bonds with increased taxes, lotteries, or even general city funds. Because of their guaranteed nature, the repaying of those costly loans has taken on a central role in many cities' budgets for years after the initial stadium deal. By shackling themselves to these massive debts (and often massive cost overruns), cities may very well have allowed the further deterioration of local schools, roads, and public services. In many cases the bond issue runs years longer than the team's lease, raising the specter of local governments, ten or 20 years hence, still having to pay off the costs of stadiums for teams that have since fled for greener pastures—or still paying off bonds on old stadiums while building new ones with even higher price tags.

Welfare By Any Other Name

For anyone who has followed the fortunes of city development policies in recent decades, this story has a familiar ring to it. Over the past twenty years, city governments large and small have made tax breaks and other subsidies a part of their regular repertoire in the drive to keep businesses in town—or lure them to relocate from elsewhere. What some have called "the economic war among the states" has its roots in the earliest years of the country (Alexander Hamilton once got a tax abatement from the state of New Jersey for starting a business there), and helped drive much early industrial development—

particularly railroad companies, which grew rich off free land grants from the federal government.[4]

It wasn't until the early 1980s, though, that the subsidy frenzy really hit its stride. As the national economy sagged throughout the late 1970s and early '80s, the country's governors and mayors became more and more desperate to retain jobs and increasingly did so by paying off companies to stay put or relocate to their region. Those years saw an explosion of local government subsidies for private investment. In 1977, less than half of all states provided tax incentives or public loans for private development; fifteen years later, hardly a state was without them.[5]

In his study "No More Candy Store," researcher Greg LeRoy detailed dozens of examples of what he called "subsidy abuse." In 1994, Baton Rouge granted tax abatements worth a total of $14,372,600 to Exxon in exchange for the company creating exactly one new permanent job. Sears accepted $240 million in land and cash bonuses from the state of Illinois just for staying put, while laying off many of its local employees.[6] Meanwhile, the automaker BMW garnered a $150 million subsidy from South Carolina for a new car factory; then Mercedes-Benz topped BMW with a $253 million tax break from Alabama for a plant that created just 1,500 jobs, meaning the state had spent nearly $170,000 for each new job.[7] Over one two-year span in the 1980s, the state of Louisiana handed out $3.7 billion in tax abatements, and denied exactly zero applications.[8]

Small cities and towns, eager to show that they could compete with the big boys, quickly leaped into the fray. In 1993, Amarillo, Texas, went on the offensive with a page from the phone companies' marketing plan: The city sent 1,300 checks, each worth $8 million, to selected companies around the country, offering to cash the check for any company that would commit to creating 700 jobs in Amarillo.[9] The following year, tiny Rio Rancho, New Mexico, outbid towns in several neighboring states for an Intel computer chip manufacturing plant, handing the chip maker $114 million in incentives and tax breaks even though the town couldn't afford its own high school.[10]

As a result of the explosion of corporate subsidies, tax breaks, according to the Economic Policy Institute, now dwarf all other state and local economic development projects combined. And as LeRoy writes in "No More Candy Store," "Despite recurring predictions that the states have finally grown tired of their ruinous 'economic development civil war,' the size of incentive packages continues to skyrocket. Whereas a package worth $50,000 per job sparked debate in the mid-1980s, by the early 1990s, there were several deals worth $100,000 to $150,000 per job and one worth $350,000."[11]

In terms of the level of public subsidies, sports teams can easily hold their own with other industries. When the first wave of public stadium-building hit in the late '60s and early '70s, stadiums were $40 million affairs, a sum that could be at least somewhat offset by rent and other fees paid by the baseball and football teams that shared these hulking multipurpose facilities. By the 1990s, though, stadium costs had soared to $300 million and up. Teams were demanding separate buildings for each sport, as well as more expensive accommodations inside—while rents had plummeted, to zero in some cases, allowing teams to keep all the new revenue from their stadium for themselves at the expense of their host cities. The Ravens' deal with Baltimore, in which the team pays no rent or construction costs and received a $50 million cash relocation fee, was extravagant but not unprecedented: The previous year, the L.A. Rams had agreed to move to St. Louis in exchange for a low rent (just $250,000 a year), while receiving all luxury box and concession revenues and 75 percent of advertising and naming rights fees—plus a $46 million relocation fee.[12] (One fellow owner was moved to call it "the mother of all stadium deals."[13]) What was once at least in part a public investment in a city's sports team had turned into an outright subsidy—and the price was getting ever steeper.

Sports stadiums and arenas don't pay for themselves—not even their staunchest advocates claim they do. Even in the 1960s and '70s, when public money was first used in a consistent fashion on sports facilities, the returns on the new buildings—increased rent and advertising, higher ticket sales and concession prices—were still not enough to offset the millions of dollars a year in debt payments by the state or city that fronted the money. And for today's buildings, with exponentially higher costs, there is no question of making them self-sufficient.

The explanation from local officials for these subsidies has invariably been that a new stadium is needed if the team is to stay in town, and that indeed a team in town is needed if the city hopes to make a great urban comeback, or remain a "major-league city." New sports facilities are highlighted by the national media in pop analyses of a city's lifebeat—thus, Camden Yards and Jacobs Field are seen as symbolic of the great revitalizations of Baltimore and Cleveland, as is Coors Field of the supposed renaissance of downtown Denver. As Indianapolis Mayor William C. Hudnut 3d told *The New York Times* right after the Colts fled to his town's new dome, "It's a wonderful thing for our community. It's a boost to the city's image nationally and to local morale as a symbol of major league status."[14]

All for One and One for All?

When it comes time to convince taxpayers to vote for new stadium subsidies, stadium proponents—whether team owners, local business interests, or enthusiastic politicians—don't just rely on images of an emotionally rejuvenated civic pride. Instead, their central argument has historically been that the new facility will mean an economic windfall for its host town.

Building a stadium at public expense—even if the teams don't pay rent or share ticket, concessions, or parking revenues—will mean long-term prosperity *and* respect, citizens are told. It's difficult to find U.S. cities, whether large or small, even with vastly different economic bases and financial prognoses, in which sports teams and their new stadiums are not continually held up as economic bonanzas, worthy of enormous public investment and sacrifice. A new arena or stadium, it is said, can jump-start a flagging economy with millions of new fans and spin-off businesses like restaurants, hotels, and other tourist attractions.

For example, an organizer of the drive to bring the Oakland Raiders football team to the city of Sacramento in the 1980s once remarked, "The Raiders coming to Sacramento would be an event of the magnitude of the Gold Rush."[15] And when discussing a threatened exodus of the New York Yankees from their historic stadium in the Bronx, New York Mayor Rudolph W. Giuliani, while publicly lamenting any move at all, crowed that a proposed West Side of Manhattan location would provide a revenue stream for the city that was "off the charts."[16]

It's a tempting offer, especially for cities that have seen other industries flee town for the suburban plains or for competing cities willing to cough up more lucrative tax breaks or a more pliable labor force. But can the numbers be trusted? That's what Cleveland community activist Marge Misak took a hard look at before the 1995 vote on her city's sin tax extension that would ultimately pay for a new football stadium.

"At the time there was a claim in *The Plain Dealer* that the mayor basically asserted that the stadium would bring $46 million in economic development to the city," Misak explains. Since the news article failed to report where Mayor White had come up with the figures, Misak went on the trail of the original source. "It turned out that it had come from an earlier study that the Growth Association, I think, of Cleveland had done.

And basically the mayor's office took this number and extrapolated it for the '95 season and came up with $46 million. Over half of that money was actually the revenue that would be generated from ticket sales and concessions at the stadium. Well, all of that money goes into the owners' pockets."

There's a difference, ultimately, and an important one, between benefit to the *economy* and benefit to the *treasury*. If people buy an extra $10 million in goods (whether cans of tuna fish or baseball tickets), that's $10 million extra for the economy, but unless it's taxed in some way, the government doesn't see any money from that.

Money for Nothing
In fact, the claim that public funding of new sports facilities leads to quick and easy urban success stories is vastly overrated, say most economists. These critics charge that, by ignoring basic economic realities and crucial issues in urban planning, the pro-construction studies are left with a central premise that is almost always out-of-whack.

"The consulting reports are basically political documents," says economist Roger Noll, perhaps the nation's preeminent sports finance expert and the co-editor of *Sports, Jobs and Taxes*, an exhaustive tome from the Brookings Institution. "Usually they're supported by the people who want a stadium, and so they come up with unrealistically high numbers. Occasionally, they're supported by people who don't want the stadium, and they come up with real tiny numbers." In fact, in study after study, when those done by local chambers of commerce and the like are thrown out, the claims of stadium boosters are resoundingly rejected.

"Given the self-serving nature of these studies," adds economist Robert Baade, the author of several definitive analyses of the topic, "I wonder if we shouldn't be looking at things a little more carefully than we are." He's devoted his efforts to doing just that. A professor at Lake Forest College in Illinois, Baade has gained national attention for his extensive examinations of the actual benefits that sports teams and new facilities do or do not bring to cities. And he, like many other economists across the country, calls into question the basic claims and priorities of new stadium deals.

One of the more extensive examinations of the issue was a 1994 study Baade did for the Heartland Institute, a think tank that opposes almost any government regulation or spending. (On its board of directors are representatives from Amoco, Philip Morris, Fidelity Bank, and Procter & Gamble.) Baade looked at 48 cities over a 30-year time span, examining every U.S. city during that period that had acquired either a new professional sports stadium or arena or a professional sports team (baseball, football, basketball, or hockey). His overwhelming finding was that "professional sports teams generally have no significant impact on a metropolitan economy."[17] Because of that research, Baade's study "finds no support for the notion that there is an economic rationale for public subsidies to sports teams and stadium and arena construction. Professional sports does not appear to create a flow of public funds generated by new economic growth. Far from generating new revenues out of which other public projects can be funded, sports 'investments' appear to be an economically unsound use of a community's scarce financial resources."[18]

Among the 30 cities with new stadiums or arenas that Baade examined, 27 showed no economic impact on their local economy over a 30-year period. In three instances—St. Louis, the San Francisco Bay Area, and Washington, D.C.— the new facilities appeared to have *hurt* the local economy.

Economists point out that even when cities do see an increase in spending because of a new stadium or the addition of a sports team, that doesn't represent new dollars flowing in to the local economy so much as expenditure substitution— money shifted from one entertainment source to another. Far from generating new economic activity, as new stadium proponents continually assert, Baade says that the new facilities at best seem to bring in dollars that otherwise would have been spent elsewhere in the immediate or general region.

"If you draw larger and larger circles away from the place where the sporting event actually occurs, it's more and more likely that you're going to have a zero sum game," says Baade. "In the case of Wisconsin, it may well be that you're taking money away from a dog racing track in Racine when you subsidize Brewers baseball. It may be that people who ordinarily go to the racetrack may now go up to Milwaukee to see a game at the new retractable-dome stadium. But you have to wonder about the implications for other entertainment activities in Racine."[19]

Sometimes the issue of displaced dollars confronts stadium backers themselves. In his push for a new home for his Denver Broncos football team, owner Pat Bowlen cited the new baseball-only stadium the city had just completed as a draw that was taking away from his now outdated facility. The local media was reporting that season ticket sales at Mile High Stadium were suffering since the baseball Rockies began play at brand-new Coors Field, and Bowlen had the answer. "Coors Field is a beautiful place to see a game," he told the *Denver Post*, "Football needs those kinds of venues to stay competitive. I have to have a stadium that's as attractive as baseball."[20] Thus, a city was in effect being told (much as had happened in Cleveland) that once it got the ball rolling on new stadium construction, it would be only fair to lay out the public dollars for each and every team in town.

Mark Rosentraub, a professor of urban planning at Indiana University, also questions the displaced dollars that sporting events take in: "How much more food do people eat because of the presence of a team?" Rosentraub writes. "In other words, if a family eats dinner near the stadium or arena before a game, where did they not eat their dinner that night?...Sports are not only small potatoes, but those potatoes may have been someone else's before the team or stadium existed."[21]

The same goes for claims of new jobs to be had from stadium spending. Minnesota Wins!, a pro-stadium group funded by the Twins, Vikings, and local corporations, estimated that a new baseball-only stadium costing $310 million would generate an additional $35.9 million in economic activity and the equivalent of 168 new full-time jobs—prompting University of Chicago economist Allen Sanderson to remark that if the money were "dropped out of a helicopter over the Twin Cities, you would probably create eight to ten times as many jobs."[22]

Moreover, the new jobs that are created are not necessarily cream-of-the-crop positions. "They're parking garage attendants, they are hot dog salespeople, they are waiters and waitresses, sometimes cooks, people who do maintenance work and repair work and cleaning," says Cleveland union activist John Ryan. "And none of them are jobs that the mayor hugs his kids and says, 'I hope you can get one of those jobs someday.'"

Rosentraub has also examined stadium boosters' promises in great detail. In a study Rosentraub did for his 1997 book, *Major League Losers*, he looked at the private-sector payrolls for all U.S. counties with at least 300,000 residents, and found that only .06 percent of the jobs in those counties were associated with either professional sports teams or managers. Noting that "if they were classified by their gross revenues, they would be considered small to medium-size businesses," he concludes that the economic impact of professional sports teams is actually quite small—especially compared to the size of the public subsidies, which can often run as high as $250,000 per job.[23]

All of which begs an even larger question: If stadium construction funds end up coming from the same civic coffers as other municipal projects, and if massive stadium deals are being given the go-ahead nationwide, what isn't getting funded instead? When Toronto built the costly SkyDome for some

$400 million, the city was having trouble coming up with money for its parks department. "One city official estimated that the city needed 700 new acres of parkland to keep pace with the demand," writes Charles C. Euchner, a political science professor at the College of Holy Cross, "but the city had a budget of just $500,000 for parks acquisition. Other infrastructure needs that went begging included public transportation, housing rehabilitation, and expansion of the sewer system."[24]

Economist Dennis Zimmerman goes a step further in emphasizing what he calls the "opportunity cost" involved in publicly funding a new stadium. "If an alternative generates $2 million of benefits net of subsidy and the stadium generates $1.5 million net of subsidy, the stadium can be viewed as imposing a $0.5 million *loss* on taxpayers, not a $1.5 million *benefit*," Zimmerman wrote in his 1996 study for the Congressional Research Service assessing, among other things, expenditure substitution in publicly funded stadium projects.

Thus, in a case such as Baltimore's construction of a new home for the Ravens, Zimmerman believes that "economic benefits were overstated by 236 percent, primarily because the reduced spending on other activities that enables people to attend stadium events was not netted against stadium spending. And no account was taken of losses incurred by foregoing more productive investments. The state's $177 million stadium investment is estimated to create 1,394 jobs at a cost of $127,000 per job. The cost per job generated by the state's Sunny Day Fund economic development program is estimated to be $6,250."[25]

It isn't as if these and other studies have been kept hidden from the public. In fact, during the early days of the latest debate in New York over a proposed new home for the Yankees, the Heartland Institute sent copies of its studies to city planners. Baade, Noll, Zimbalist, and others are quoted constantly and often called upon to testify at legislative hearings on the topic, and yet the frantic pace of new stadium construction continues. It's interesting to see how the stadium builders themselves justify the economics of new stadium construction—because if local municipalities aren't benefitting from new stadium deals, as the research indicates, these people certainly are.

The Dirty Dozen

For a look at the stadium builders' response to the economic studies, one need only have attended the Inaugural Municipal Issuers' & Sports Franchises' Symposium on Sports Facilities Finance—a long-winded title for a conference largely devoted to reassuring those who benefit from new sports facilities that their business is alive and well. Filling the conference room at Manhattan's Grand Hyatt Hotel for the two-day conference in May 1997 was a who's who of sports industry movers and shakers: municipal officials, stadium authority employees, team executives, and financiers from across the country, all gathered to hear how to profit from new stadium construction. Jerry Colangelo, whose sports empire had recently grown to three Phoenix-area pro franchises, was the keynote speaker. And featured on the program, along with such panels as "Remodeling vs. Building a New Stadium" and "Beyond Peanuts and Crackerjacks: Examining Unique Revenue Streams," was what looked to be the owners' long-awaited counterstrike to the Baades and Rosentraubs of the world: a panel entitled "Letting the Numbers Speak for Themselves: Public Funding and Economics." "This panel," a program note promised, "will finally answer the age-old questions, not with anecdotal opinions but with actual numbers derived from detailed studies."

With the crowd still buzzing from Colangelo's lunchtime address, James McCurdy, president of the low-minors Pioneer Baseball League, took the podium. "I'm not going to talk about numbers," he drawled. "I want to talk to you about how you think about numbers"—then reeled off a monologue on "paradigm paralysis versus paradigm pioneers" that would not have been out of place at any motivational seminar, and that, as promised, steered clear of any economics at all. McCurdy did, however, manage a dig at economist Mark Rosentraub, calling him "the Howard Stern of the stadium business," drawing a few chuckles from the otherwise stone-faced crowd.

McCurdy's pep talk complete, Philadelphia commerce director Stephen Mullin stepped to the mike. "Are cities getting conned?" he asked. "Are sports teams worth it? Are subsidies too high?" How much benefit do stadiums really have, he asked the crowd rhetorically, then answered his own question: "I don't know, but I think it is positive."

With that, Mullin dropped the subject of economic benefits of stadiums. As did the conference as a whole, which spent its remaining hours mulling how best to get cities to go along with new stadium plans. The only "detailed studies" presented were Rosentraub's, which were presented by panelist Joseph Passafiume of Buffalo's county government, to deafening silence from the assembled onlookers.

Cities' willingness to believe the claims of these stadium boosters, despite all evidence to the contrary, reminds Robert Baade of Pascal's Wager. "The idea was somebody asked if [French philosopher Blaise Pascal] believed in God, and he said, 'Yes, I believe in God because I can't take a chance that there isn't one.'" Baade says. "I think in some ways that resembles city attitudes with regard to this thing. I think that people who make decisions about these things say to themselves that we believe there is an economic impact because we really can't take the chance that there isn't one. In part I think that's a reflection of the state of urban America."

3 BALL BARONS

"Anyone who quotes profits of a baseball club is missing the point. Under generally accepted accounting principles, I can turn a $4 million profit into a $2 million loss, and I can get every national accounting firm to agree with me."
—TORONTO BLUE JAYS VICE PRESIDENT PAUL BEESTON[1]

"Deep Throat was always right: Follow the money."
—SPORTS ECONOMIST RODNEY FORT

When *Financial World* magazine conducted its yearly roundup of the sports business in 1996, it advised would-be investors to keep an eye out for teams that met three criteria: "The revenues they rake in from their venues are below the average for teams in their sport, they have no definite plans to build or move into a new facility, and their leases expire by 2000 (or can be rather easily gotten out of)."[2] Anyone buying into one of these "undervalued" franchises—the poor, stadiumless, and mobile—could see their investments skyrocket in value, the magazine advised, by levying a build-or-else ultimatum. Topping the magazine's to-buy list: the Hartford Whalers, which were projected to double in value if moved to a new publicly funded arena in Nashville.[3]

The sports industry is relatively small by the standards of the corporate world—"about the size of the pork and beans industry," in the memorable words of former Senator Sam Ervin.[4] But for the handful of men (and still tinier handful of women) who own major-league sports franchises, it's very big business indeed. Since professional sports began, running a team has always been a reasonable investment, likely to earn an owner a tidy return of a few percentage points a year. In the 1980s, though, according to James Quirk and Rodney Fort's masterful study of sports economics, *Pay Dirt*, franchise values in every sport abruptly leaped upward: baseball teams by 23 percent a year, football by 19 percent, and basketball by an astounding 50 percent—meaning an NBA team bought during that decade would likely double in value in less than two years.[5]

There's a pleasant myth that in the early days of pro sports, teams were run by gentleman owners, whose concerns lay more with performing a civic duty for their local community than with turning a profit. The story has a grain of truth—as late as the 1970s, most sports franchises were owned by independent moguls, some of whom could trace their families' ownership back to the early 20th century—but even they kept a firm eye on the bottom line. And by the 1980s, independent owners had begun to give way to even more profit-conscious corporate ownership.

The first prominent sports team to come under corporate ownership was the New York Yankees, bought by CBS in 1964 (making the old gibe that "rooting for the Yankees is like rooting for U.S. Steel" uncomfortably close to the truth). CBS divested itself of the team in 1973 (selling it to a Cleveland shipbuilder named George Steinbrenner), but the television network was ahead of its time: By the 1990s, even most wealthy individuals were being priced out of the market: With franchise values soaring past the $100 million mark, ownership of a sports franchise had passed from being a privilege of the rich to one of the super-rich.

Today, those reaping the rewards of the sports value boom include such corporate conglomerates as Disney and Time-Warner, for which a sports team is just another item in their portfolio. The independent owners who remain are those who can afford the high-stakes world of modern-day sports—billionaires like Carl Pohlad of the Minnesota Twins or Microsoft cofounder Paul Allen, who owns the Seattle Seahawks football team and the Portland Trailblazers basketball club. For those who can afford the entry fee, the payoff can be staggering.

Ballpark Figures

When discussing sports finances, the first thing to understand is that the numbers literally don't add up. Without an understanding of the inner financial workings of the sports industry, it's impossible to comprehend the most obvious conundrum of modern pro sports: Even as revenues soar to record levels, team owners invariably insist that they are losing money hand over fist. Contract negotiations with players' unions, in particular, have occasioned especially shrill cries of poverty, with management insisting that any concessions from their side of the table will plunge them into bankruptcy, or even result in teams disappearing altogether from the face of the map. "It will take a club to go belly up in order to stop this madness," Montreal Expos general manager Dave Dombrowski warned ominously just before baseball management giveback demands helped spur players toward an eight-month-long strike in 1994 that cost owners hundreds of millions in lost revenues—and which was immediately followed by the leagues' decision to expand by two teams in 1998.[6]

None of this is unexpected or unusual, especially in an industry faced with relatively powerful unions ready to leap on any scrap of profit growth to boost their own salaries. But unions and others skeptical of the owners' claims can point to a statistic that belies the owners' poverty claims: Sale prices of teams are soaring, and even a break-even or money-losing team is likely to yield a huge financial windfall for its owners once they decide to put it up for sale. As baseball owner Bill Veeck once explained, "You don't make money operating a baseball club. You make money selling it."[7]

When examining public subsidies, it's important to remember that not all are simple cash handouts. In fact, most corporate welfare, in any industry, comes in the form of tax breaks: special dispensations to evade local, state, or federal taxes that can save corporations or wealthy individuals millions of dollars. Whenever the federal government allows deductions for one group and not for another—for homeowners but not for renters, say, or for sports franchises but not for other businesses—the subsidy may be hidden, but it's just as real as if Congress were doling out cash from the federal treasury.

For sports owners, tax breaks have been an integral part of doing business ever since they discovered perhaps their most incredible financial gimmick, the depreciation of players. This trick was first devised in the late 1940s by then-Cleveland Indians owner Veeck, an innovator and iconoclast who at one time or another owned three different major-league baseball teams. It was Veeck who introduced some of the most popular ballpark events of his day: As a Chicago Cubs executive, he planted the ivy that to this day distinguishes Wrigley Field's outfield walls; he held the first-ever Bat Day; he built Comiskey Park's famed exploding scoreboard; and in his most famous gimmick, he sent a midget up to bat (Eddie Gaedel walked and was promptly removed for a pinch-runner). It's less well-known that he also devised a plan to buy the last-place Philadelphia Phillies and import players from the Negro Leagues, five years before Jackie Robinson broke baseball's color line, but was blocked by league authorities.[8] (Veeck later bought the Cleveland Indians and promptly signed the

American League's first African-American ballplayer, Larry Doby.) Veeck was much reviled by his fellow owners for his antics, but it was he who first discovered the accounting scheme that would change the face of the pro sports business: the notion that player contracts could be depreciated, just like industrial equipment, providing a potentially huge tax deduction for owners by turning an actual profit into a paper loss.

The sharp-eyed Veeck had noticed that a 1935 IRS ruling had allowed cash purchases of players to be written off as an expense of running a sports business—athletes could be considered just another spare part that wore out and ultimately had to be replaced. What if, he wondered, he were to treat the acquisition of a team's entire roster at the time of purchasing a team in the same way? Better still, by declaring nearly all of a team's value to reside in its player contracts, an owner could depreciate nearly the *entire* purchase price of a team over several years.

On the face of it, this argument is absurd. Most athletes, after all, *increase* in value as they gain experience, at least until age takes its toll. What's more, teams already claim the costs of player development—scouting, minor-league teams, and the like—as a business deduction, and claiming both depreciation and replacement cost deductions is usually a sure way to raise red flags at the IRS. Yet the tax agency would instead turn out to be remarkably understanding over the years. Depreciation of player contracts quickly caught on in all four major sports, and was soon standard operating procedure for all teams. When Paul Beeston of the Toronto Blue Jays bragged that he could turn a $4 million profit into a $2 million paper loss, he wasn't just making a bargaining point with labor; he had an eye to the millions in tax benefits that the paper loss could earn his team.

In 1970, Rodney Fort became one of the first researchers to challenge the fiction that players were a major part of the value of a sports franchise and as such could be depreciated until the team's "value" had all but disappeared. Milwaukee car

dealer Bud Selig had bought the fledgling Seattle Pilots baseball team, which had finished dead last in its only year of existence, for $10.8 million and moved them to Milwaukee, where
they became the Brewers. Fort recalls how Selig's tax documents assigned a value of $10.2 million to the players them-
selves, meaning that fully 94 percent of the purchase price
could be written off as depreciation. "I was working with Roger
Noll, and we were as generous as we could possibly be in figur-
ing out the relative value of this team to all the rest of the
kinds of players in the league at the time," says Fort. "We came
up with something like three million, tops. The judge read it,
said, well, that's a good piece of work, but I can see no reason
that Selig's choice violates the accepted rules of accounting in
Major League Baseball."

With that invocation of the "accepted rules," the Veeck
loophole stood—meaning team owners in the four major
sports could continue to reap huge rewards from this tax break.
Although its benefit was reduced somewhat by the 1986 Tax
Reform Act, the depreciation bonus continues to earn teams
tax savings; and if depreciation isn't enough, plenty of other
loopholes remain for enterprising owners to fall back on. For
one thing, they can deduct interest payments on loans they
take out to buy the team; better still, owners can create dummy
corporations to own their teams, lend *themselves* money, and
then deduct the interest payments that the teams pay back to
themselves. Team owners who have their own television sta-
tions—as franchise prices soar, more and more teams find
themselves owned by media conglomerates—can sell themselves their broadcast rights at bargain-basement prices, creating yet another book loss.[9]

The list of fiscal shenanigans is endless, including the $2
million in parking and concessions fees that Anheuser-Busch,
owner of the St. Louis Cardinals baseball team, diverted to
another subsidiary in 1984; and the $25 million that New York

Yankees owner George Steinbrenner reportedly paid himself in the early 1980s as a "fee" for negotiating his team's cable contract.[10] When Roger Noll was hired by the Players' Association to look into baseball's books in 1985, he determined that what Major League Baseball had claimed was a $41 million industry loss was in fact a $25 million gain.[11] For sports teams, Quirk and Fort conclude, "The balance sheet and the income statement simply lie in describing the financial health of the team, as they do with the typical tax shelter operation."[12]

Why the federal government allows this kind of accounting to continue is "the ultimate unanswered question in sports," according to Fort, who continues to follow the sports industry from his position in the Washington State University economics department. But then, notes Fort, baseball's famous antitrust exemption, in place since 1922, has a similarly hazy legal footing—and a similarly cynical explanation. "The IRS is, after all, an administrative agency," he says. "And even though none of those guys are elected, the choices they make do have political impact. And so I can envision elected officials thinking, make baseball teams 15 to 20 million bucks poorer with the stroke of a pen, in a seemingly volatile financial situation, and all hell's gonna break loose. And so the IRS is probably instructed by the political overseers not to do that."

Suite Deals

When sports owners talk about old stadiums lacking the "amenities" of the new ones, they're not speaking of high-tech scoreboards or spacious player clubhouses, though the newest buildings are flush with those as well. By and large, there's one thing that distinguishes new sports facilities from old ones in terms of profit-making potential: luxury boxes.

The Houston Astrodome, which in 1966 brought the world Astroturf and indoor baseball, was also the first stadium to offer "skyboxes," a ring of luxury suites nestled against the building's roof. Despite the bird's-eye view, they were an immediate sellout. Luxury boxes quickly became a fixture in the new public ballparks of the '70s, and by the '90s were a primary element of ballpark architecture. A luxury box in Philadelphia's Veterans Stadium (built in 1971) is architecturally functional, enjoying such customary amenities as private elevators and separate stadium entrances. But in structure and luxurious feel it's quite clearly more than 20 years old—nothing like the lavish boxes in Cleveland's Jacobs Field, with their spectacular views of the city skyline and attention to all the modern amenities corporations have come to expect from recreational outings in the 1990s.

Over the course of the 20th century, the world has been introduced to night baseball, basketball's three-point shot and instant replays in football and hockey, but no innovation can match the luxury box for sheer money-making power without improving either the quality of the game or the enjoyment of the average fan. Along with their cousins the "club seats"—sort of an open-air corporate suite of prime seats with expanded legroom and waiter service—luxury boxes are about money, pure and simple. By the 1990s, teams were charging more than $100,000 a year for the private suites. This was money that didn't have to be shared either with the teams' municipal landlords or with their fellow owners, since all four major sports exempt suite revenue from profit-sharing among teams. With upwards of 200 boxes in some of the newest stadiums, this can translate into millions more a year in team profits.

The vast new revenue streams made possible by luxury boxes, in fact, have driven much of the current wave of stadium construction, as even relatively new facilities are declared "obsolete" for lack of suites (or enough of them). The stadium-building boom of the '80s and '90s was a huge boon to sports teams' bottom line, as each box took what would have been a

few dozen moderately priced seats and turned them into a previously unheard-of source of lucrative income.

But luxury boxes constitute more of a subsidy than just the
public money spent on building the glassed-and-carpeted
enclosures themselves. The key here is the target market,
which for luxury boxes—and the majority of club seats—consists overwhelmingly of corporations. When an average fan
plunks down $25 for a ticket, the money comes straight out
of his or her pocket, but when a corporation buys tickets, the
finances work differently. Companies are able to claim sports
tickets as a business-entertainment deduction, on the theory
that this is a perk they use to lure clients, wining and dining
them in an attempt to land business deals. Because of this, so
long as a company has profits to declare the deduction
against, it can rest assured that the federal government will
pick up the tab for a portion of the purchase price. Team
owners can then safely charge more for their boxes, knowing
that corporations will happily pay higher rates if the purchase
is tax-deductible.

This is a subsidy that's seldom included in figures on public
spending, yet the rewards for team owners can be substantial.
For example, take a stadium with 100 luxury boxes, each selling
at $80,000 a year—not at all out of the ordinary for the lavishly
appointed structures of today. That's $8 million that corpora-
tions are spending every year on boxes, of which 50 percent is
deductible, saving them about $1.2 million in federal taxes.
Multiplied by the 7,000 or so luxury boxes currently in use in
the United States, the luxury-box subsidy costs the federal treasury more than $80 million a year in lost tax revenue.

The size of the subsidy used to be even larger: Until the mid-
1990s, 100 percent of business-entertainment expenses could be
deducted, and that change to the tax code did, in fact, take a
good bit of steam out of luxury box sales. But it by no means
stopped them entirely, as corporations continue to take advan-

tage of this tax shelter; some teams, in fact, make a point of distributing brochures to their corporate clients detailing the best ways to use luxury box purchases to reduce their taxes.

The Ten Percent Solution

Yet another hidden subsidy lurks in the fine print of stadium deals. When cities finance these projects, they do so with federally tax-exempt bonds. Since the bond buyers don't have to pay taxes on their income from these bonds, municipalities can sell them at lower interest rates. This reduces the cost to the city treasury (since it has to pay less in interest each year), but it comes at the expense of the federal treasury, which forgoes taxes on the bond buyers' profits. As a result, stadiums look cheaper than they really are, with the federal government kicking in the difference.

Tax-exempt bonds have been around ever since the introduction of the federal income tax in 1913. For decades, cities and states levied these bonds, which can be sold at a much lower interest rate because they are tax-free, generally for roads or other public works. But beginning in the 1950s, cities started using tax-exempt bonds for economic development projects by private industry. By the early '80s, so-called "private activity" bonds were everywhere—amounting to nearly 80 percent of all government bonds issued, and soaking up so much capital that there was little left over for genuine public-interest projects. So Congress made a point of eliminating this subsidy as part of the 1986 Tax Reform Act, making private activity bonds subject to the usual taxes. And in what was intended as a death blow to public stadium deals, lawmakers specifically declared sports construction projects to be private activity and thus taxable.

They left two loopholes, however. First, since no elected official wanted to be accused of sabotaging his or her own city's bid for a sports team, the tax reform bill contained a grandfather clause exempting all stadium and arena projects then under way, as well as a list of 26 other projects that were merely under consideration. This clause would go on to create billions more in federal subsidies.

The other loophole, though unintended by its congressional drafters, ultimately proved far more lucrative to team owners. The Tax Reform Act had redrawn the definition of private-activity bonds to be exceedingly strict: Any bonds where more than ten percent of the use would be by a private entity, and where more than ten percent of the bonds would be paid off by revenue from the private project, were considered taxable. But what if the stadium lease were drawn so that total government revenues—whether from lease payments, ticket surcharges, parking fees, or whatever—were held below that ten percent threshold? The local government issuing the bonds would take a bath on them, for sure. But if a city's political leaders were willing to go along, teams could still have the use of tax-exempt bonds—and a guaranteed 90 percent of the resulting revenues to boot.

The difference between taxable and non-taxable bonds may sound trivial, but it adds up quickly. Because interest rates on tax-free bonds are significantly lower, and because interest payments wind up constituting the lion's share of the cost of a bond-financed projects, stadiums can be built far more cheaply—albeit by the federal government forgoing its tax revenue on the bonds. The lifetime federal tax subsidy on a stadium financed with tax-exempt bonds can be as high as one-third of the total cost.

New York Senator Daniel Patrick Moynihan, who had helped craft the 1986 law, was appalled at how his envisioned tightening of the tax laws had been turned into the biggest loophole yet, in effect forcing cities to fund only facilities that were guaranteed money-losers. "In other words," Moynihan would later explain before Congress, "non-stadium governmental revenues (i.e., tax revenues, lottery proceeds, and the like) must be used to repay the bulk of the debt, freeing team owners to pocket stadium revenues. Who would have thought that local officials, in order to keep or get a team, would capitulate to team owners—granting concessionary stadium leases and committing limited government revenues to repay stadium debt, thereby hindering their own ability to provide schools, roads, and other public investments?"[13]

But that's exactly what cities did, in droves. Stadium rents, which had previously been used to defray at least part of the cost of a publicly built stadium, plummeted, as municipalities struggled to keep revenues below the ten percent threshold. This, explains Maryland Stadium Authority deputy director Ed Klein, was the origin of the lease discrepancy that would cause friction between the Orioles and Ravens: While the Camden Yards baseball park (built under the 1986 loophole) could safely charge rent to the baseball team, the new Ravens football stadium couldn't without running afoul of the new limit. Instead, the Ravens were granted free rent, which immediately sent the Orioles clamoring for a free-rent deal to match. "The Tax Reform Act of 1986 was in theory supposed to put an end to these [stadium deals]," observes Roger Noll, "but all that it did was reduce the rents to zero."

Congress had created a monster. The law that was supposed to put a stop to stadium giveaways had instead caused them to metastasize. Moynihan would later try to close the loopholes he had created, but as of 1997, he had still been unable to convince his congressional colleagues to pass a bill eliminating tax-exempt bonds once and for all.

What's in a Name?

As if direct subsidies and tax loopholes weren't enough, there's yet another way for sports owners to make money at public expense. This is the diversion of revenue streams (in sports business parlance, every source of cash, from tickets to popcorn to advertising signage, is considered a "revenue stream" in the team's ledgers) that would otherwise benefit the building's owners—the local government—into the owners' corporate coffers. The newest cash cow on the block is naming rights—for a fee of up to $60 million, corporations can affix their name to a stadium, guaranteeing unlimited exposure during every sports telecast or news recap. And though the stadium itself may be owned by the public, the fee invariably goes straight into the team owner's pocket.

There's hardly a stadium under construction that doesn't bear a corporate moniker, from Pacific Bell Park (San Francisco) to Miller Park (Milwaukee) to Bank One Ballpark (Phoenix). Even older facilities can be renamed for a fee—San Diego's Jack Murphy Stadium, named for a renowned local sportswriter, became Qualcomm Stadium at Jack Murphy Sports Complex after a computer company kicked in $18 million; and Cincinnati's Riverfront Stadium will end its days promoting the local power company as Cinergy Field. With old stadiums, though, there's always the danger of the new name not taking (Candlestick Park's transformation into 3Com Park, for a local computer company, was short-lived, as public disdain for the new name led to the official adoption of "3Com Park at Candlestick Point" as the park's name), and besides, who wants to advertise on an aging billboard when a brand-new one can be had the next town over?

With the exception of Pacific Bell Park, which is being privately built by the Giants, all these stadiums are publicly owned. Yet naming fees nearly always go to pay the teams' share of construction costs, and are not counted as public subsidies.

Ballparks Go Condo

Owners have likewise captured the bulk of revenues from the other great innovation in sports money-making: personal seat licenses. Since the dawn of professional sports, team owners have juggled ticket prices up and down, trying to balance their desire for increased profits with their fear of alienating fans.

Occasionally, there would be attempts at ticket surcharges and other hidden fees, but these extra charges seldom amounted to more than another dollar or two—until, that is, the invention of personal seat licenses (PSLs). These devices burst onto the sports scene in the early '90s as a new way of raising funds directly from the fans themselves, and in so doing substantially raised the ante on what level of subsidy teams could demand.

The first proto-PSLs appeared in Texas Stadium, the football stadium built by Dallas Cowboys owner Tex Schramm for his team in 1968; Schramm offered 40-year "seat options," allowing fans to buy—and sell—their season ticket rights. PSLs then disappeared for nearly 20 years before their rediscovery by Max Muhleman, a sportswriter-turned-marketer who, in 1987, stumbled upon the idea while searching for a way to raise money for a new arena that the Charlotte Hornets basketball team was hoping to finance without public funding. His solution: Sell "charter seat rights" to fans, guaranteeing them a shot at scarce season tickets in exchange for a nonrefundable fee.

"We thought as an incentive to season ticket holders who were being asked to put up forfeitable deposits that they be given what we thought every fan would always like to have— and that was essential ownership of their seats," Muhleman explained in a 1996 newspaper interview. "Instead of the team dictating who could have your seat if you moved out of town or whatever—in some cities you couldn't give the seat to your buddy and in some cases couldn't transfer your tickets to a family member if there was a waiting list—we thought it would be nice to designate these as seat rights that could be held by the original ticket buyer."[14]

Six years later, North Carolina businessman Jerry Richardson was looking for an edge in his competition for an NFL expansion franchise. The going was rough: Other cities like St. Louis and Baltimore had new stadiums on the drawing boards, while Richardson had been unable to convince

Charlotte to build one for him. Muhleman proposed raising $100 million for a stadium via his charter seat license gimmick.

The licenses, by now renamed "permanent seat licenses," sold out the day they went on sale. This time, the close-knit cabal of sports owners sat up and took notice. Richardson, much like Bill Veeck four decades before him, had abruptly discovered a whole new revenue stream for sports teams—all you needed was a new stadium, and a few thousand fans desperate enough to get their hands on tickets to invest $1,500 or more in a PSL.

PSLs are an especially devious money-making tactic because of their hybrid nature. Not quite a ticket surcharge, not quite an investment, they can be used to lure fans into paying far more for sporting events than they would otherwise. If fans decide to give up their season tickets, they are told, they can sell their PSLs to another buyer and be out only the cost of the tickets they've already used. If they're lucky—if the team is doing well, say, and demand for tickets is high—they may even reap a profit. "It has been unfairly reported that a seat license is a surcharge on top of your season ticket, or simply a charge that you have to pay before you have a right to buy a season ticket," said Muhleman in 1996. "In fact, what you are buying is control that ordinarily rests entirely with the clubs."[15]

It's the kind of win-win scenario that sounds more fitting for a pyramid scam than for a multimillion-dollar investment—and for good reason. PSLs are an investment, but one whose value depends entirely on the willingness of someone else to buy that "control" from you. For 10-, 20-, or 30-year "personal seat licenses" there is at least an expiration date built in; buyers know that the licenses will be worth little toward the end of their useful life—who wants rights to a season ticket for only a year or two? But even for so-called "permanent seat licenses," such as those being sold for the San Francisco Giants' planned new ballpark, the permanence lasts only as long as the team stays put. With teams now staying in a facility for a decade or two at most, a 30-year PSL could end up being no more real an investment than a Ponzi scheme, with PSL owners at the time the team moves left holding the bag.

The profits from PSLs, meanwhile, almost always go directly to the teams, regardless of whether it's the team or local government that owns the seats themselves. One of the few examples otherwise—the Oakland Coliseum—provides an indication of some of the pitfalls of relying on fans' speculation on seat rights to raise capital for a stadium.

The Oakland Raiders had led the wave of NFL franchise relocations in the '80s, leaving behind a rabid following in Oakland for the larger market of Los Angeles in 1982. But by decade's end, owner Al Davis was already itching for a better deal. After hearing pitches from such unlikely suitors as tiny Irwindale, California, Davis focused his attentions on none other than Oakland, which had never given up hope of luring the Raiders back to their original home.

Davis' price was steep. In exchange for the Raiders' return, he would demand that 22,000 new seats be added to the Oakland-Alameda Coliseum at public expense—along with two 40,000-square-foot clubs and 125 new luxury suites. (The resulting wall of seats would tower precariously above the rest of the bowl-shaped stadium, peering out at passing motorists like a transplanted slice of some other building entirely.) Since the city of Oakland was in no position to raise the necessary $100 million on its own, city officials turned to PSLs as their savior. Upon the Raiders' return, the city announced, anyone wishing to buy season tickets would first be required to pay a fee of up to $16,000 for a 10-year personal seat license.

But by opening day of the 1996 season, when the Raiders made their triumphant return by losing 9 out of 16 games on the year, the Oakland Football Marketing Association, the nonprofit organization set up jointly by the Raiders and the city to push PSL sales, had sold just 35,000 of the 45,000 licenses, leaving the city $35 million in the hole for the already-completed construction. The marketing association, desperate to fill the newly expanded stadium, began selling tickets without requiring a PSL purchase first—and soon enough faced the added obstacle of a lawsuit, filed by a fan who had purchased a PSL back when they were being sold as the only way to get a Raiders season ticket, and who now charged the city with fraud.

Despite the controversy, personal seat licenses—variously called permanent, preferred, premium, or charter seat licenses—continue to flourish, especially in football, where high ticket prices are already common and a short season keeps tickets in high demand. In each case, the main beneficiary is almost always the team; even when PSLs are used to defray the cost of building a stadium, they are generally considered part of the team's contribution toward the project.

"Private" Stadiums, Public Cost

Naming rights and PSLs are only the beginning of indirect subsidies to sports teams, which are as varied as the stadiums and arenas that they help finance. Pacific Bell Park, in addition to its naming rights deal, is an example of yet another hidden subsidy. Though construction of the ballpark will be privately financed (by PSLs, naming fees, and the private sale of taxable bonds), the cost of clearing the land for the facility will be paid for by the city of San Francisco—an additional $1.2 million a year. Other stadiums, such as the Washington Redskins' new privately built football emporium in southern Maryland, have likewise taken what's been dubbed the "offramp" approach to subsidies, raking in hundreds of millions of dollars in government expenditures for new highways, roads, and parking lots around the new facility. And there's always the opportunity for additional subsidy via tax breaks: When the owners of the New York Knicks and Rangers threatened to leave town in 1982, the city agreed to exempt whatever corporation controlled the team from *all* local property taxes so long as the teams stayed put—a clause that has cost the city millions of dollars in tax revenues as the teams have been passed from hand to hand among larger and larger corporations in the ensuing years.[16]

As public opposition to sports giveaways grows, teams and municipal governments are growing more and more adept at playing hide-the-subsidy. Arenas are especially susceptible to this trend. Because of their smaller size and greater income capacity (a well-utilized arena can be full 365 days a year with hockey, basketball, and concerts, as opposed to baseball's 81 home games or football's eight to 12 Sundays), arenas are more likely to be financed with private money—ten of the 13 sports facilities built privately since 1987 have been arenas. But scratch the surface of even these deals, and you'll find public involvement: The "privately built" Fleet Center in Boston sits atop a $100 million city-funded parking garage; Philadelphia's $217 million CoreStates Center (built next door to the 29-year-old Spectrum in 1996) included $32 million in state funds. Overall, about 40 percent of new arena construction winds up being financed by the public.[17]

Lastly, there are always ticket guarantees, whereby localities promise to reimburse teams for unsold seats. When the San Diego Chargers football team intimated in 1996 that it was thinking of relocating when its lease expired in 2003, the city agreed to spend $76 million on renovating city-owned Jack Murphy (now Qualcomm) Stadium and adding 10,000 seats. City officials also guaranteed that for the next ten years, at least 60,000 tickets would be sold for each game, with the city making up any shortfall.

It was only after the deal was signed that critics pointed out an odd consequence of this ticket guarantee. Because the Chargers' renegotiated lease called for the team to pay ten percent of ticket revenues to the city as rent, owner Alex Spanos would stand to earn 90 percent of the face value of all tickets sold. For tickets unsold, however, the city had agreed to pay the team *100 percent* of the ticket price—meaning the Chargers would make more money *not* selling tickets than selling them. Since the team's lease did not limit what Spanos could charge for these tickets, the team's owner had a potentially limitless pipeline to the city treasury.

When local libertarian activist Richard Rider realized what the city had agreed to, he was aghast. "It became apparent when this came up that the city council, and we think even the city manager who negotiated the deal, didn't know what they'd done," he says. "They get their ten-year guarantee, without any control over the prices. And we're building 10,000 seats that basically nobody wants. The real reason for doing the stadium remodeling is to come up with skyboxes. But the 10,000 extra seats are seats nobody will use."

Rider predicts that the total city subsidy could easily wipe out the Chargers' $5.5 million in yearly rent, leaving the city paying the team to play before a near-empty house. "A good parallel to think of is the airline industry," Rider continues. "One thing an airline doesn't want to fly is an empty seat. You want to sell out your industry. So they do whatever they have to do—they cut all kinds of deals, they're constantly juggling their prices trying to sell them. Well, we just told the Chargers that it's actually not important for you. In fact, it's less than not important—it gets better."

Anatomy of a Swindle

If the benefits of a major-league sports team are insufficient to repay a city for constructing a new stadium, as Robert Baade and his fellow researchers argue, they're nowhere near enough to compensate for all the various subsidies that a new stadium can earn its sports tenants as well. Take a sample stadium—say, the TWA Dome in St. Louis. Built in the early 1990s to lure an NFL expansion franchise to town (thus filling the football vacuum left when the Cardinals were lured away to Phoenix in 1988), the new dome was bypassed in favor of Charlotte and Jacksonville, leaving the city desperate to lure an existing franchise to relocate. In 1996, they found one—the Los Angeles Rams—but at an astronomical cost to taxpayers.

The TWA Dome was constructed entirely at government expense, with $301 million raised by selling general-purpose bonds. That $301 million, plus interest, will be paid back at $24 million a year over 30 years; a boost in the county hotel tax will pay for about a quarter of the sum, and the rest will be paid out of the general city and state treasuries. The 113 luxury boxes and 6,500 club seats will generate $1.8 million per year in tax subsidies via the business-entertainment deduction, paid for by the federal treasury. U.S. taxpayers will likewise be responsible for an additional $6 million a year in subsidies through the federal tax exemption of the bonds. Trans World Airlines agreed to pay $1.3 million a year (plus inflation) to plaster its name on the dome, nearly a million of which will go to the Rams. Total subsidy: $1.07 billion over 30 years.[18]

That amounts to a public cost of $36 million a year, while the Rams' annual revenues are expected to leap by more than $15 million. And according to the team's brand-new lease, if the stadium does not remain among the most lavish in football for another ten years, the Rams can then leave town for more lucrative turf—or demand further improvements.

4 THE ART OF THE STEAL

"The subsidy they get is totally disproportionate to the economic benefit they bring.... It would ashame Jay Gould and his fellow robber barons of the 19th century. Even Genghis Khan got sated after awhile."
—HOUSTON MAYOR BOB LANIER, EXPLAINING WHY HE HAD OPPOSED PUBLIC FUNDING FOR A NEW STADIUM FOR THE HOUSTON OILERS FOOTBALL TEAM, AUGUST 1996[1]

"The result [of not using public funds] is that we won't have any pro sports in Houston. Things might change some day, but the reality is that if you say [no to public subsidies] in today's market, you're below any market."
—LANIER, EXPLAINING WHY HE WAS SUPPORTING PUBLIC FUNDING FOR A NEW STADIUM FOR THE HOUSTON ASTROS BASEBALL TEAM, OCTOBER 1996[2]

Stadium deals can bring unprecedented riches to a sports team owner, but city residents tend to be unenthusiastic at first. "Sure, we love our team," is a typical response when the stadium juggernaut rolls into a new city. "But hundreds of millions of dollars for rich owners and greedy players, when we can barely even afford to buy books for our schoolkids? It'll never fly."

Yet fly it does, in city after city. Regardless of how vocal the public opposition or how cash-strapped the municipal treasury, rare is the local government that has just said no to the demands of its sports franchises. Before a stadium proposal hits the drawing boards, polls will show that even though people don't want to see their team leave town (no surprise), neither do they want their tax money spent to keep them; yet invariably, these *nos* turn to *yeses* by the time public referenda are held. Nearly every city has some local politicians who proclaim that public funds will be spent on a new sports facility over their dead bodies; by the time the bond issues are passed and ground is broken at the construction site, they will likely as not be the ones wielding the shovels.

This pattern has been followed in cities large and small, those run by Democrats and Republicans, by free spenders and those traditionally stingy about every penny:

• Houston Mayor Bob Lanier's disdain for the sports industry didn't stop at comparing team owners unfavorably to Mongol hordes. In the midst of Oilers owner Bud Adams' fight for a new football stadium, Lanier commissioned a study that found that the entire sports industry in Houston, plus all other events at the Astrodome, amounted to less than one percent of the city's economy—smaller than the total economic impact of the Houston Medical Center.[3] In 1995, Lanier let the Oilers pack up and leave rather than accede to their demands. Yet within just a year of that team's announced departure, the city, county, and state had agreed to team up behind a $465 million construction project for new baseball and football facilities, while making plans for a new basketball arena as well.

• When the Seattle Mariners threatened in 1995 to leave town if they didn't get a new baseball stadium to replace the 19-year-old Kingdome, Seattle voters narrowly rejected a referendum calling for public financing for a new stadium. But state legislators, not to be deterred, held a special emergency session to authorize the $320 million in funding anyway—then raised the figure to $414 million when the Mariners complained.

• Detroit had a historic ballpark in Tiger Stadium, a 30-year lease with its baseball team, and a 2-1 public vote against spending city funds on a new stadium. It also had a well-organized opposition that had convinced the state legislature to deny any state funds for new stadium construction. But though it took ten years and a change of team ownership to make it happen, the mayor and governor ultimately were able to find $320 million to tear down and replace Tiger Stadium—and plan a separate downtown stadium for the Detroit Lions as well.

• Four times between 1987 and 1992, San Francisco–area voters were asked to approve public money for a ballpark for the San Francisco Giants. Four times, the referendum was presented as the "last chance" to keep the team in town. And four times, the voters turned the Giants down flat. Finally, the Giants' owner, a multimillionaire real estate heir named Bob Lurie, tried to sell his team to new ownership in Tampa, only to see his own fellow owners reject the deal. The Giants were ultimately sold to local supermarket baron Peter Magowan, who decided to build a new park almost entirely with private funds, and San Francisco looked to have gotten away with standing up to stadium black-mail—until the 49ers football team demanded, and received, $100 million in public money toward a stadium/mall complex to replace Candlestick Park.

If you're a sports owner looking to have your city build you a new stadium at public expense, the obstacles can initially seem daunting: Public opposition is a given, and getting government approval can be even worse—even when elected officials are on your side, the political process can drag on for long, luxury-box-deprived seasons. To smooth the path, owners and their political allies have devised a set of strategies to coerce elected officials, media reporters, and taxpayers into accepting the necessity of a multimillion-dollar subsidy for their local sports millionaire. If you're an owner looking for a windfall of public money, follow this game plan, and you, too, can pull a last-second victory from the jaws of defeat.

Step 1: The Home-Field Disadvantage

When trying to convince taxpayers of your need for a stadium, there's an obvious obstacle: You already have one. Because of this, the first step is usually the *obsolescence claim*—alleging that your old stadium is obsolete, insufficient to cater to the demands of modern fans, or even on the verge of physical collapse.

"They say, 'The old girl, she's getting old. I love that place as much as anybody, but...'" says Frank Rashid, co-founder of the Tiger Stadium Fan Club, which has spent a decade battling two different pizza barons over the fate of the Detroit ballpark. "Whenever anybody says that, you know, watch out."

Rashid should know, because he's watched some masters of the obsolescence claim at work. In 1987, Tigers owner Tom Monaghan (also the owner of Domino's Pizza, and a leading supporter of the anti-abortion group Operation Rescue) claimed that it would cost up to $100 million to effectively repair 75-year-old Tiger Stadium; when Rashid's group investigated, they found the actual figure to be a mere $6 million.

At the same time, America's oldest ballpark, Comiskey Park on the South Side of Chicago—built in 1909 as one of the first steel stadiums in the country—was similarly declared obsolete. As in Detroit, the White Sox owners hired an engineering firm to study the feasibility of renovating Comiskey; the old ballpark passed every test the engineers threw at it (including piling 50-gallon drums of water in a stadium concourse to see if the floor would give way), but the study recommended tearing it down anyway. The owners also may have decided to help it along some: By many accounts, from the time owners Jerry Reinsdorf and Eddie Einhorn purchased the team from Bill Veeck in 1981, hardly a single penny was put into maintenance of the ballpark.[4]

Several hundred miles to the northwest, meanwhile, citizens of Minneapolis could look on their neighbors in Chicago and Detroit and breathe a sigh of relief that they were through with such squabbles. The downtown Hubert H. Humphrey Metrodome might not be the most beautiful edifice in the country—Yankees manager Billy Martin once wondered aloud, after watching his fielders losing flyballs in the glare of the translucent fabric roof, how they could "name someone like Hubert Humphrey after such a dump." But at least it was new, built in 1982 to house the baseball Twins and football Vikings, costing the citizens of Minneapolis some $55 million. It was also fresh and modern, a domed stadium built at the height of dome fever—a time when St. Petersburg dome booster Richard Dodge could say, "There is something about a dome that excites people, they get more bullish on themselves and where they live. It gives them a new and positive view of themselves. They react to issues and challenges in different ways. You can say it is the pride factor."[5] Old Metropolitan Stadium out in suburban Bloomington, roofless and unloved, was dynamited in 1985, its demise filmed for use in a disaster movie, and was replaced by the world's largest mall.[6]

Eleven years later, the fashion pendulum had swung to old-time parks like Camden Yards, and the antiseptically modern Metrodome suddenly looked positively archaic. The Twins, noting that a minor-league team across the river in St. Paul was outdrawing their club on warm summer days, decided that an unroofed stadium was what they needed after all. Or perhaps a *retractable* roof, like those tried in fellow cold-weather cities Toronto and Montreal—though the former city's dome had gone more than $300 million over budget, and the latter's was stuck permanently in the closed position. Minnesotans, who were still paying a sales tax surcharge to finance the bonds for the old new stadium, were faced with picking up the tab for a do-over.

Shortly after the Twins presented their demands, the Minnesota Vikings football team suggested that they should get a new stadium as well.

In Houston, the Astrodome, dubbed the Eighth Wonder of the World when it was built in 1966, was abandoned by its football tenants in 1995, and the eponymous Astros demanded a new open-air downtown park the following year. Basketball and hockey arenas have been even quicker to be thrown on the scrap heap. In 1986, Denver spent $12.5 million renovating McNichols Arena—just 11 years old at the time—for the Nuggets basketball team, improving the scoreboard and adding new luxury boxes and restaurants. Eight years later, city arena manager Gary Lane was calling the boxes "spartan" and "claustrophobic," and the Nuggets were demanding a new facility.[7]

Next door to the Nuggets, Denver Broncos owner Pat Bowlen chimed in that his football team's home, Mile High Stadium, was rusting and might fall down.[8] "This is a serious, serious question," said Bowlen in asking for $180 million in state money toward a new stadium. "Where do we play in 1998 or 1999 if that stadium is condemned?"[9] As in Detroit, independent engineers countered that Mile High was in fine shape; one declared that the stadium could "last indefinitely" if properly maintained.[10] What was not in perfect shape, it turned out, was Bowlen's bank account—the owner had sold the rights to Mile High's luxury boxes some years earlier to raise some quick cash, and hoped that a new stadium would restore the millions a year in luxury-box revenue that he had sold off.

Meanwhile, the shifting sands of stadium tastes have left cities scrambling ever faster to keep up with the latest trends. The owners of the Pittsburgh Pirates, who left 35,000-seat Forbes Field in 1970 for the publicly financed 50,000-seat concrete bowl of Three Rivers Stadium, approached the city in

1996 with demands for a new publicly built facility. The new stadium should be a "35,000-to-37,000-seat park with natural grass and no roof, bells, or whistles," owner Kevin McClatchy said. And one more thing—perhaps it could be modeled after Forbes Field?[11]

Step 2: Faking a Move

"That isn't even on the table, on the agenda," proclaimed Philadelphia Eagles owner Jeffrey Lurie to the press corps that had assembled for the opening of Eagles training camp in 1996. Lurie, responding to rumors that the team would relocate to Los Angeles, insisted, "It's never even been discussed. It's so off the map....I know it sells papers and I know....I lived in [Los Angeles] for nine years and I know you can sell a story quickly by saying, 'Uh, the team could be moving to L.A.' Forget about it. The fans can feel very, very safe that this franchise will be very successful in this area."

"And," as the *Philadelphia Daily News* remarked the next day, "with those three little words—'in this area'—Lurie perked up the good listeners in the room while opening up another can of worms."[12] Because "this area," they knew, could mean across the river to southern New Jersey, which had already offered to build a new arena for Philadelphia's basketball and hockey teams.

Successfully threatening to pick up and move a sports franchise to another city is an art form unto itself, one that you need to perform well if you're to achieve the proper goal. Lurie brandished a few more tricks of the stadium trade in his speech to the press that summer day in Philadelphia—he also noted how sports teams "spin off tremendous economic benefits" and warned ominously that "I'm not going to allow this franchise to get in the kind of situation Art Modell got into in Cleveland"—but with his opening words, he proved that he had mastered the basic ingredient of sports welfare brinkmanship: the *non-threat threat*.

Even the most casual follower of the sports industry can tell you that teams get their demands met by threatening to move to other cities; and yet, virtually no owners ever make that threat themselves. Those who are too direct about the threat risk getting slapped down by angry local politicians and columnists, as San Francisco 49ers president Carmen Policy found out after bluntly threatening to leave town if an upcoming stadium-funding referendum was not approved. His statements made front-page headlines and stunned even 49er supporters—"I almost shit when I read it," gulped state senator John Burton—and Policy quickly had to back away from the overt threat.[13]

Somewhat tempered words, like those used by Lurie, are more effective in conveying the proper mix of hometown spirit and subtle blackmail. As Miami Heat executive Jay Cross told his fellow sports leaders following his team's successful campaign for a new basketball arena, "We never threatened. We never said we're going to leave. When people asked us what we're going to do if we don't win the referendum, we said, 'We don't know. We don't know where we're going to play. We don't have a choice. We'll have to look around.'"

The undisputed master of the non-threat threat is George Steinbrenner, whose 20-odd-year tenure as owner of the New York Yankees (with time off for one felony conviction for illegal campaign contributions to Richard Nixon's Committee to Re-Elect the President, and one suspension for hiring a gambler to spy on one of his players) has been little more than one long plea for a new city-financed ballpark.[14] Despite being universally reviled even by his own team's fans as a meddling blowhard, Steinbrenner has managed to put himself in position to reap an incredible $1.2 billion stadium in the heart of Manhattan—all without a viable threat to move.

When Steinbrenner, an heir to a shipbuilding fortune, bought the team from CBS for $10 million in 1973, it was about to move into a newly renovated Yankee Stadium (really rebuilt from the ground up), with 25 luxury boxes and a state-of-the-art scoreboard, all thanks to $125 million in state and city funding. The administration of Mayor John Lindsay had agreed to the reconstruction, in response to threats by the team's then-owner, CBS, to move the team to neighboring New Jersey.

Steinbrenner was happy with his new stadium until the early '80s, at which point he dusted off the old New Jersey threat and demanded further renovations. Although New Jersey voters have shown little enthusiasm for building him a stadium, Steinbrenner's demands have steadily escalated: from minor renovations, to a complete "old-time" reconstruction of Yankee Stadium—with such publicly funded amenities as a new commuter rail station, an additional bridge across the Harlem River to Manhattan, and a new parking lot built by paving a nearby public park—to a brand-new ballpark in mid-town Manhattan that would cost $1 billion or more.

If anything tarnishes Steinbrenner's record, it's that he has yet to get his dream stadium for his efforts. Before the start of the 1996 season, he declared that he would make a decision on where to move the team by Opening Day; he repeated these words before the start of the 1997 season, then leaked word to the press that negotiations would be put on hold until after the mayoral election, in which Mayor Rudolph Giuliani, a supporter of the $1 billion Manhattan plan, was expected to face one of two staunch stadium opponents.

Unspecified threats can prime the pump of public spending, but when it comes time to win an important vote, owners invariably bring in the big guns: the sports league presidents and commissioners, who are pressed into service to warn of the consequences of a no vote. When then-baseball commissioner Fay Vincent made his trip to Cleveland to warn that a no vote on the Indians stadium would mean no Indians for Cleveland, it was just one in a long string of last-minute appearances by league executives to try to pull victory from the jaws of defeat. In Houston, it was National League president Leonard Coleman who delivered the dire warnings during talks on a new stadium for the Astros in 1996: "We want to do all we can to first keep a team in Houston," Coleman told reporters. "However, if we cannot strike some kind of agreement with regards to stadiums…I don't think we would ask a businessman to lose millions of dollars each year."[15] Bud Selig, the Milwaukee Brewers owner who became "permanent acting commissioner" when Vincent was fired by the baseball owners, got to deliver the threat in Minnesota three weeks before that state's legislature decided whether to fund a new baseball stadium, declaring that "if there isn't anything on the horizon to change the economics, baseball will allow that club to move. We'll have no alternative."[16] A week after Selig's visit to Minneapolis, American League president Gene Budig announced his support for a new stadium for the Boston Red Sox, saying, "No one is anxious to leave Fenway Park, [but] it is important here that we be realistic in terms of economics and the long-term viability of the Boston Red Sox."[17]

Threats, of course, are easy. But the obvious question then is, will the teams really follow through if a city says no? Details are sketchy—in part because so few cities have called their teams' bluffs—but there are indications that some sports franchises' threats to hit the road may be more idle than they would have voters believe. Both the Detroit Tigers and San Diego Chargers played the threat card while in the middle of long leases that would have been difficult if not impossible to break. The Houston Astros successfully threatened a move to Northern Virginia in 1996, even though no stadium funding was forthcoming in that state, and Baltimore Orioles owner Peter Angelos was reportedly preparing to file suit against any team that tried to relocate on his doorstep.[18]

Finding a prospective suitor, in fact, has become more and more difficult in recent years for teams looking to create leverage for a new facility at home. For years, for example, baseball owners' favorite tease was Tampa Bay, a relatively large metro area (20th-largest in the United States) with a stadium (the publicly financed Florida Suncoast Dome, since renamed Tropicana Field in a naming-rights deal) but no major-league team. Over the years, the San Francisco Giants, Chicago White Sox, Texas Rangers, Cleveland Indians, and Baltimore Orioles all threatened to move to Tampa if they didn't get their way; all but the Giants ultimately won new stadiums from their current hometowns.

But it is the nature of modern sports leagues to expand (thanks to the $100 million–plus fees that expansion-team owners must pony up to the existing teams to gain entrance to the major leagues), and in 1995, Major League Baseball granted Tampa Bay an expansion franchise to begin play in 1998— the Devil Rays.[19] With Tampa no longer on the horizon to bully their cities with, teams had to resort to such new locales as Charlotte, Sacramento, Portland, Oregon, and the Virginia suburbs of Washington, D.C. No one dared mention that some of these cities were not even considered worthy candidates for expansion by the leagues.

"We make fun of these 'free-agent franchises,'" says economist Rodney Fort. "Well, if there really were such things, all of the league owners know that that's bad for business. You've got to cultivate that longstanding relationship with fans and the identity and the tradition and all that jazz." Not to mention wanting to hedge your own bets—as University of Illinois law professor Stephen Ross observed when Minnesota Twins owner Carl Pohlad was threatening to move his team, "If you're an owner and thinking, 'What are my options?' you don't want [Pohlad to move to North Carolina] because then *you* can't threaten to move there."[20]

How the different leagues handle this tension between the desire to play the move threat and the need for stability has varied, Fort notes. Ever since Al Davis survived an NFL lawsuit and moved the Raiders to Los Angeles in 1982, the football league has approved all proposed franchise shifts without a challenge. (The league did make the Rams pay a $65 million fine for moving from a more lucrative TV market in Los Angeles to a smaller one in St. Louis, but then approved the move without a vote—and the city of St. Louis wound up paying the fee, in any case.)

"Then you look at baseball," continues Fort. "There hasn't been a move, although there have been lots of threatened moves, since 1972, when the [Texas] Rangers opened up shop. I think there's two differences. One is, there's a lot more cities out there willing to host a football team. The NFL for some reason hasn't been quite as good at expanding into those places that are real viable threats to existing team hosts. Either [baseball has] been much better at it, or the owner group is so cohesive that they've watched the Al Davis episode, and they have some blood-brother agreement in there that they're just not going to do that to themselves."

Fort and his colleague James Quirk recently looked at how well leagues did at saturating the top 30 U.S. population centers with teams; baseball, Fort says, was the hands-down winner. "So part of the story then, we think, is [that baseball is] just better at keeping a few cities around to use as this ploy so that they do have some viable alternatives out there to use as leverage against existing franchise hosts. But not so many that an individual owner is going to look around, and the payoff is going to be so large that they'll bolt."

In the end, says Fort, each league's strategy may prove successful. "Major league baseball chooses to expand, keep the number of cities at a manageable level so that they still have some threat. The NFL chooses not to expand as much, given the pressure for teams, let the teams move around a little more, and then expand and fill in behind them—which is doubtless going to happen in L.A. and Cleveland. Maybe after the fact, in terms of league revenues, either of those strategies works okay." But in either case, one constant remains: While leagues will allow teams to use cities for leverage all they want, there's no way they'll abandon a lucrative market outright.

Step 3: Leveling the Playing Field

If voters aren't swayed by fears of falling girders or fleeing ball-clubs, your next step is to plead fairness: The team simply can't be competitive in the existing stadium. Virtually every owner in every sport has used this appeal, but as Rashid points out, they're seldom clear on exactly what it means—"competitive on the field, or the business is competitive, or what. But it suffices, because nobody asks what they mean by it. There's never a follow-up question."

"The economics of professional sports today is that, without a facility, you really can't compete," Phoenix baseball, basketball, and hockey owner Jerry Colangelo told a reporter in 1997. "And if you can't compete, you can't get support. And if you can't get support, you go out of business."[21] Not literally, of course—in fact, despite recurrent warnings of impending doom by sports owners, no major-league team has folded in over 30 years. Yet the mere threat of a team falling into second-class status has been enough to strike fear into the hearts of politicians and fans alike.

This is where the owners' cooked books really come in handy. One favorite gambit of owners is to release an "audit" of team finances that purports to show massive yearly losses. In November 1996, Orioles owner Angelos released a report claiming $6 million in yearly losses, despite the team's league-high attendance and sweetheart lease. Earlier that same year, the stadium-hungry Astros released an audit that claimed the team was losing over $20 million a year.[22] But since Major

League Baseball prohibits teams from opening their books publicly—and privately held corporations have no obligation to make their tax records public—there's no way to verify the numbers. Owners thus have the best of both worlds—they get to parade losses before the media, while claiming that league rules prevent them from providing any hard details.

Baseball, in particular, has been the site of fierce debate over the gap between "have" and "have-not" franchises; with the freest free agency of any major sport (other leagues have salary caps imposed to prevent player contracts from being bid up too high), it is argued, it's far too easy for a rich team like the Yankees ($133 million in yearly revenues) to buy up all the best players, while low-revenue teams like the Pittsburgh Pirates ($40 million in yearly revenues) must rely on younger, cheaper, less talented players.[23] (Baseball owners rejected a plan to share more revenue between rich and poor teams in 1994, helping lead to that year's disastrous player strike.) A new stadium is a way to level the playing field, teams like the Pirates have argued, and indeed, several teams (the Cleveland Indians being the prime example) have seen remarkable on-field improvement coinciding with the opening of a new stadium. In fact, the correlation often seems too coincidental: Several teams have started collecting higher-paid players in the years when stadiums are still in construction, leading to some speculation that small-market owners may keep their teams on a tight budget on purpose to help promote their argument that a new ballpark is necessary for the team to compete for a pennant.

What's more, even when a team in genuinely dire economic straits cries for "competitiveness," there's a problem: What one team has, its rivals immediately want as well. So when a small-market team—say, the Baltimore Orioles—gets a lucrative new stadium, its big-market rivals like the New York Yankees demand an equally lush facility. Since the Yankees' other revenue, primarily TV and radio contracts, dwarfs those of teams like the Orioles—and baseball's relatively weak revenue-sharing plan means the Yankees' owner can keep the bulk of this local income without sharing it with other owners—it will then be time for the Orioles to once again cry for "competitiveness" and demand further concessions from their host city, beginning the cycle anew. In fact, those claiming that they need a new stadium to compete have included the owners of the richest franchises (Yankees owner Steinbrenner, whose team rakes in an estimated $24 million in profits per year) and some of the richest men in the world (Twins owner Carl Pohlad, whose family wealth is well over $800 million).

In the NFL, where revenue sharing is much stronger—in particular, TV contract money is shared across the whole league—the tactics used by teams have been somewhat different, notes Fort. "I haven't seen an NFL team go to a local government and say, 'I'm losing money.' They go to the city and say, 'In order to be competitive, I have to get more non-shared revenue sources. So if you want me to go to the Super Bowl, you've got to give me a new stadium, with gobs of luxury suites.'" Ironically, this may make football teams even hungrier for new facilities, since unlike TV and ticket revenues, income from stadium-based revenue streams like luxury boxes and PSLs don't have to be shared with their fellow owners, making a new stadium one of the few sure ways for owners to put money directly in their own pockets.

Step 4: Playing the Numbers

At this point, it's time to pull out those consulting reports documenting the boundless benefits that will befall your city should it grant you a new stadium. If possible, get your friends in government to commission these reports—no point, after all, in paying for anything you don't have to, and local governments have proven eager to fund studies justifying their desires to build new sports facilities.

Baltimore's dual-stadium project alone spawned a mountain of support documentation; nearly every year saw another thick tome appear from some governmental study group. After hundreds of pages of minutiae on such items as population growth and sports magazine circulation by region, each reached the same conclusion: Build something. By the time of the groundbreaking for the football stadium, Maryland Governor Parris Glendening could declare confidently that the project would result in 1,400 new jobs and $123 million annually to Maryland's economy, and know that somewhere in the amassed paperwork were figures claiming to confirm it.[24]

The numbers themselves here almost don't matter. Predictions of economic benefit, in fact, are all over the map—which should come as no surprise, given that they all amount to little more than guesswork. But even clearly specious numbers can serve an important public relations purpose. In every city where team owners have won a public vote on a new stadium, a key factor has been the claim that the facility will cost taxpayers little or nothing—or that any cost will be made up for by the resulting boost to the local economy.

The plan to build a new football stadium for the San Francisco 49ers provides a striking example of this. The $100 million in city money that would be required, the team explained, would help create 10,000 jobs in the neighboring community of Bayview-Hunters Point. And best of all, the stadium would come with an attached mall, which, it was claimed, would generate more than enough tax revenue to pay back the city's share of the costs.

Two separate economic impact studies by city officials failed to confirm the team's promises: One projected a near break-even for the city; the other concluded that expenditure substitution from other shopping areas would cost the city $4.6 million a year in lost taxes.[25] Yet the claims served their purpose: The team was able to promote its stadium as a boon not just for the football team, but also for the surrounding neighborhoods and the city as a whole—a strategy that worked to perfection when the stadium referendum squeaked through on the strength of overwhelming support from Bayview-Hunters Point voters.

Step 5: The Two-Minute Warning

No matter how well you've played your cards to this point, there's always the danger that the proceedings may threaten to drag on indefinitely as pesky voters demand referenda or legislative leaders hit gridlock in deciding on a funding plan. At this point, you may want to declare a crisis: Proclaim that the window of opportunity on a new stadium will only remain open for so long, leaving unstated what disaster will befall the city if the window should be allowed to slam shut. Rashid calls it the "used car salesman" approach: Buy now, because this offer won't be good for long.

Not only can a false crisis jump-start a stalled stadium deal, it can also be repeated as necessary. Astros owner Drayton McLane's stadium negotiations with Houston were a bizarre series of cascading deadlines, each one more "final" than the last. The ploy began with William Collins, a businessman from the Washington, D.C., suburbs who was rumored to be interested in buying the club. "Mr. Collins has made it clear that he hopes to have baseball in the Virginia area by 1996," Astros Vice President Bob McClaren said in October 1995. "Common sense would say to us that in the next four to eight weeks, they would have to have something in place."[26] No new construction plans were in place in Houston by then, but neither were they in Virginia, where Collins had run into a wall of opposition for his own demands for a publicly built stadium. McLane bided his time for a while, then issued a new deadline: August 1. When D-Day finally came—preceded by increasingly apprehensive media reports—McLane promptly granted another extension. The deadlines didn't stop until mid-

September, by which time the local government finally gave in to McLane's demands.

There have even been crises that the participants later admitted to faking to boost public concern. When the Detroit Tigers, in 1991, gave Wayne County executive Michael Duggan an August 1 deadline, no one publicly questioned it. Only later did Duggan reveal that the deadline was his idea—he had, in effect, told the Tigers to blackmail him.

Five years later, Rashid recalls, the Wayne County Board of Commissioners was to decide whether to dedicate still more money for a new stadium for the Detroit Lions football team. Rashid and fellow activist Kim Stroud watched as Duggan presented the board with, in Rashid's words, "hundreds of pages of stuff that they had to read in a matter of a few days and then make a judgment on. They were begging for more time. No matter how they felt about the project, they said, basically, we spend more time determining matters that involve tens of thousands of dollars—this is something that's going to involve hundreds of millions of dollars. We don't have time to study this."

The board approved the money, only to watch as the stadium process dragged on for months more as city and teams haggled over the site and the financing. "There was no rush," says Rashid. "The need for the rush was to avoid public scrutiny."

Step 6: Moving the Goalposts

Once you have successfully gotten your stadium on the drawing board, your task is not over—far from it. As any owner knows, the deal struck with your local government on a new sports facility is only the opening gambit. Cost overruns are a certainty, especially if you have plans for technological novelties like a state-of-the-art retractable roof. In any case, since you have the upper hand in renegotiations—you can always change your mind and leave in the middle, after all, but a city can't do much with a half-built stadium—you are free to renegotiate the terms of the deal again and again if you like.

In San Diego, for example, when the $66.6 million expansion of Jack Murphy Stadium went over budget (among other things, the stadium had been built on sandy soil, leading to problems in earthquake-proofing), the city quickly agreed to raise the additional cash, selling the stadium's naming rights to computer company Qualcomm for $18 million. "The trick is to get the deal going," says San Diego stadium opponent Richard Rider. "Once it's going, you say, 'We can't quit now!'"

When the city of Toronto first planned the stadium-and-hotel complex known as SkyDome in 1985, estimates were that construction costs would be in the neighborhood of $150 million (Canadian), with the city and the province of Ontario kicking in $30 million apiece. In fact, the stadium, complete with the world's first working retractable roof, would ultimately clock in at a whopping $600 million (roughly $500 million in U.S. dollars), the second most expensive sports facility in North American history. (Number one in that category: Montreal's Olympic Stadium, built in a hurry for the 1976 Olympic Games, which cost $1 billion Canadian and features the world's first *non*-working retractable roof.) As a result, SkyDome was a hit with fans and tourists but a disaster for its government owners: In 1990, the new stadium's first full year of operation, the Blue Jays drew a record 3.9 million fans and turned a profit of $13.9 million; SkyDome, meanwhile, saddled with its enormous bonding cost, lost $39 million.[27]

Desperately looking for a way to reduce the $60,000 a day in interest building up on the SkyDome bonds, the province of Ontario had two choices. It could pay off the debt immediately, reducing treasury reserves in order to eliminate the incredible interest payments; or it could sell the stadium for whatever cash it could, in an effort to get rid of this massive money-loser. Bizarrely, the province did both, first writing off the debt, and then selling the now debt-free SkyDome to private interests for

$173 million. The cut-rate sale of a stadium that was finally making money would cost the province more than $45 million more in forgone income.

The ultimate stadium wheel-and-deal, however, took place in Milwaukee over several years in the early '90s, as Brewers owner Bud Selig managed to take his own promise to build a privately funded stadium for his ballclub and turn it into one of the biggest public bailouts in urban planning history. One Wisconsin lobbyist would later call the whole process "one of the fanciest pieces of parliamentary maneuvering I've ever seen."[28]

The dance began in 1989, when Selig approached Milwaukee elected officials, asking for permission to build a privately financed park on state land. Only one problem: The land in question had a highway running through it, state highway 41, which would have to be moved at a cost of $6 million. The Greater Milwaukee Committee agreed to move the highway if Selig would pay for the stadium.

Five years later, Selig approached Wisconsin governor Tommy Thompson, already then gaining a national reputation for slashing state welfare benefits, with a new dilemma: He couldn't afford to build the stadium himself. At first, Thompson proposed a statewide lottery to raise the money, similar to that which funded Camden Yards; that plan, however, was rejected nearly two-to-one by Wisconsin voters in 1995. Thompson made sure that his next gambit wouldn't be subject to any messy public votes: He asked the state legislature to hike the sales tax by one-tenth of one percent in a five-county area around Milwaukee. When the state senate twice voted down the sales tax hike by one vote, state senator George Petak entered Governor Thompson's office; at 2 a.m., Petak emerged to announce he was changing his vote. Three hours later, at five in the morning, the state senate approved the tax increase.

Enraged constituents petitioned for a recall election on Petak. (He would be recalled the following June, and immediately hired by Thompson as associate director of the Wisconsin Housing and Economic Development Agency.) But the deal was seemingly done: The five-county sales tax would provide $160 million, and the Brewers would chip in $90 million of their own funds. Even this, however, proved too much for Selig to handle. While $40 million would come from the sale of naming rights to the stadium to Miller Beer (Thompson obligingly vetoed an anti-smoking bill to avoid angering Miller's parent company, Philip Morris), the source of the other $50 million remained a mystery throughout the months to come.[29]

Selig was in a bind; even if he wanted to borrow the money himself, he was blocked by Major League Baseball limits on the amount of debt a team can carry. So Selig instead asked the state to borrow the money *for* him, using tax-exempt bonds to lower the costs of interest payments by $2 million a year. "This does not mean taking one cent more from the taxpayers," announced Metropolitan Milwaukee Association of Commerce chair Robert J. O'Toole. This was true enough if he meant only Milwaukee taxpayers, but that $2 million a year would instead come out of the federal treasury, which would be giving up income tax revenue from the federally tax-exempt bonds.[30]

Although the $50 million state loan was ultimately rejected, Selig still was let off the hook—that portion of the money was instead divided up among loans from the city of Milwaukee and from local foundations and business leaders. In the end, Selig would be responsible only for the $3 million in yearly loan payments, plus $1.1 million a year in rent.[31] And because the state also agreed to pay the Brewers $3.85 million a year for "stadium maintenance," the Brewers owner and baseball commissioner, the much-reviled man who to avoid settling a strike had cancelled the World Series for the first time ever, will ultimately receive his new ballpark virtually as a gift from the people of Wisconsin, just ten years after promising to build one himself.[32]

Step 7: Review Steps 1 Through 6

Follow these rules well, and you can count on receiving a gift-wrapped stadium or arena sitting under your tree within a Christmas or two. The San Francisco 49ers found that out—despite many PR debacles along the way, their combined use of all the tactics in the stadium-seekers' playbook, from economic promises to predictions of on-field doom to the move threat, ultimately won them a $100 million subsidy from a city that had previously denied every request for public sports subsidies.

San Francisco Examiner columnist Stephanie Salter compared the 49ers' pitch for a new stadium to that of a door-to-door salesman: "Good morning, madam. You have five minutes to do what I say. Buy this vacuum cleaner. Never mind how it works. I've explained it to the Chamber of Commerce. It's a great deal. Trust me. And if you don't buy it, I'm going to come back on Sunday while you're in church and bust up your old vacuum cleaner....Furthermore, madam, it may look as if my main purpose is to get you to buy this vacuum cleaner, but, trust me, my needs are inconsequential. Your welfare is why I'm here."[33]

5 DEUS EX PIZZA

"The city has been so desperate for something new. They want something new that's going to look good from the Goodyear Blimp. I almost think that if they built a pyramid at the foot of Woodward Avenue on the riverfront, people would get excited."
—BILL DOW, TIGER STADIUM FAN CLUB

"I have little patience with people who are paid that well wanting us to spend hundreds of millions of public dollars so that they have a nicer place to take a shower."
—FRANK RASHID, TIGER STADIUM FAN CLUB[1]

Of all the citizen groups that formed in response to move threats by sports teams, the one that garnered the most media attention may have been the least typical: Save Our Browns, the spontaneous fan movement that burst forth during Cleveland's battle over its football team. It was everything that sports fanatics are supposed to be: equally furious at fly-by-night owners and impotent politicians, and desperate to keep the team in town no matter the cost.

In truth, though, sports fans are a varied bunch, and their lives extend far beyond just following their favorite teams.

They are also taxpayers, parents of school-age children, residents of neighborhoods that would be affected by stadium-siting plans. Despite politicians' claims that "the public" would crucify them if they allowed a sports team to leave town, public opinion surveys have shown overwhelming opposition to building new sports facilities at public expense, at least until the owners rev up their media campaigns.

In recent years, stadium proposals have brought together numerous citizen activist groups from across the political spectrum to ask why residents should lose either their teams or their wallets. They have included everything from social-justice activists who advocate spending public money on schools instead of stadiums to foes of any government spending whatsoever. All, though, have returned to the same arguments when confronted with the prospect of a new multimillion-dollar sports facility to be built at public expense: It's too expensive, it isn't needed, and above all don't ask the public to pay for it when the people benefitting will be among the richest in the nation.

Of all these citizen groups, the one that stands out for its longevity, if nothing else, is the Tiger Stadium Fan Club. These were fans, all right—but as two local millionaires would learn over a decade of public battles, they were fans with a vengeance.

Queen of Diamonds

It was a September night in 1987 when five friends gathered at Buddy's Pizza in northeast Detroit to talk over the looming demise of their city's ballpark. Sitting around the table that night were Mike Betzold, a reporter for the *Detroit Free Press*; Jerry Lemenu, an illustrator and courtroom sketch artist whose cartoons often appeared in local newspapers; Bob Buchta, a local photographer; Kevin Rashid, a poet who worked days as a groundskeeper at a local college campus; and Kevin's brother Frank, a professor of English at nearby Marygrove College. As they sat eating pizza and listening to the baseball game on the radio, the five lifelong Tiger fans mulled over how to protest what they saw as the needless destruction of a cherished landmark.[2]

Tiger Stadium was just three years younger than baseball's oldest ballpark, Chicago's Comiskey Park—it had opened for business on April 20, 1912, tying it with Boston's Fenway Park as the second-oldest baseball stadium in existence—but the site's history went back a good deal earlier. Pro baseball had first been played at the corner of Michigan and Trumbull, just a few blocks west of Detroit's downtown, in 1896, when the Tigers' owner covered the cobblestones of the city's Woodbridge haymarket with sod and erected an L-shaped wooden grandstand. That original wooden park was torn down and built anew in steel in 1912, then enlarged again by the team's owners in 1936. The final result was a 55,000-seat structure that would house some of the best teams, and most devoted fans, in baseball, consistently averaging in the top half of league attendance figures year after year.

But following the Tigers' 1968 championship, local business and political leaders began making noise about joining the first wave of public stadium-building, which was then in full swing. They set their sights on a new dual-sport dome on the Detroit waterfront to house both the Tigers and the football Lions, which shared Tiger Stadium at the time. Wayne County, which encompasses Detroit and its western suburbs, actually got as far as issuing $126 million in bonds for the dome before a pair of local activists sued the city and won, arguing successfully that the bond issue had been fraudulently presented—the county had led voters to believe the bonds were backed entirely by stadium revenue, when in fact county taxpayers would be liable for paying any shortfall. The bonds were called back, and the dome died on the drawing board.

Shortly afterward, the Lions football team relocated to the new Silverdome in suburban Pontiac, and the city of Detroit pumped $18 million in renovations into Tiger Stadium, financing the work with a 90-cent ticket surcharge. The stadium's old dark-green wood seats were replaced with garish orange-and-blue plastic ones, and aluminum siding went up over the grey masonry outer walls. But the thousands of inexpensive bleacher seats were still intact, as were the memories of generations of fans. And the Tigers, unlike the Lions, still played downtown.[3]

But almost before the paint was dry from the stadium's refurbishing, rumblings began in city political circles about tearing the place down. The ballpark was too old, it was said, structurally unsound, insufficient for the needs of a modern sports franchise. As the stadium steamroller geared up once more, Tiger Stadium seemed destined to join the list of historic ballparks that had fallen beneath the wheels of progress.

Act One: Rusty Girders

As Betzold, Lemenu, Buchta, and the Rashids gathered in the fall of 1987 to discuss the fate of their home-away-from-home since childhood, they understood the uphill battle they faced. In addition to being rabid baseball fans, the five were also experienced political activists: Mike Betzold had been a leader in local nuclear freeze circles; Jerry Lemenu and Frank Rashid had worked for a local civil rights group; and Kevin Rashid had helped spearhead a doomed campaign to stop garbage incinerators from being placed in city neighborhoods. Betzold and Lemenu were also longtime contributors to *Fifth Estate*, a well-respected anarchist newspaper based in Detroit. Saving Tiger Stadium seemed like a fun way to combine their passions for baseball and social activism.

"We decided to start this thing a little bit on a lark," recalls Frank Rashid, who still lives on a tree-lined block not far from where he grew up on Detroit's inner west side. After moving into his current home, Rashid discovered that Clyde Manion, an obscure Tigers catcher from the 1920s, had lived there after retiring from baseball; photos of Manion and a young Frank Rashid, each in catcher's gear, now face off across a hallway in the house.

He and his friends, Rashid notes, all regular attendees at Tiger games since the early '60s, knew few details apart from the fact that their beloved stadium was facing a date with the wrecking ball. "We didn't want the stadium to go without a fight," he explains. "We didn't know a lot about public financing at the time—we thought it was crooked, we thought it was crazy. But we just didn't know an awful lot about it."

Calling themselves the Tiger Stadium Fan Club, the five set out to drum up support among fellow fans. By pooling their savings, they were able to scrape together enough money for 1,000 bumper stickers and 200 T-shirts reading SAVE TIGER STADIUM. In the waning days of the 1987 season, as the Tigers drove to the American League East pennant, the small band of diehards could be found each night standing outside Tiger Stadium, handing out blue-and-orange bumper stickers to anyone who would sign their club's mailing list.

The initial response was overwhelming. Hundreds of people sent in a $10 membership fee. At the Fan Club's first public meeting in January 1988, 300 people packed the small brick Gaelic League Irish-American Club, a short drive down Michigan Avenue from the stadium, to form committees to fight the demolition. By the time the 1988 season opened, the rapidly growing group had decided to stage a group "hug" of the old ballpark to mark its 76th birthday; 1,200 people gathered in a cold rain to encircle the stadium, then filed into the ballpark to present the team's grounds crew with a giant birthday card signed by hundreds of supporters. Fan Club member Mike Gruber, a *Detroit Free Press* reporter who had been brought into the group by his college classmate Frank Rashid, had loaned $20,000 of his own money for the publicity campaign for the hug, helping pay for printing a 24-page souvenir program detailing Tiger Stadium's history, and full-page newspaper ads urging fans, "Don't Let Them Make The Biggest Error in Baseball."

It was a popular sentiment at the time. Polls consistently found two-thirds of Detroiters favored simple renovation of the old stadium over replacement, and 64 percent of local residents opposed the use of city funds for a new stadium. Even team owner Tom Monaghan, the Domino's Pizza czar who had bought the Tigers in 1983, seemed to like the old ballpark, insisting at every turn that he would love nothing better than to keep the team right where it was. Asked on one occasion whether he was angling for a new ballpark, Monaghan replied that he wanted no such thing, but would go along with whatever local politicians decided: "I'll let them build a new stadium, then I'll cry."[4]

Behind the scenes, though, Monaghan was telling local politicians that he desperately wanted out of Tiger Stadium, which was, he insisted, out-of-date and decrepit, despite the recent renovations.[5] The politicians dutifully repeated his claims—particularly longtime mayor Coleman Young, the former union activist who as mayor had become a staunch advocate of city subsidies to private developers.

The first major skirmish in the battle over Tiger Stadium came in January 1988, when the Tigers announced the results of the engineering study they had commissioned the year before to "determine the costs of shoring up [Tiger Stadium's] long-neglected foundation and superstructure."[6] This was the study that, the Tigers claimed, had found the existing ballpark in need of $100 million worth of repairs. In particular, the team charged, salt spread in the aisles during snowy Lions football games, in the years before that team moved to the suburbs, had severely corroded the building's steel girders, requiring costly repairs. "Our perspective is that the stadium isn't going to fall down tomorrow, but this grand old lady is getting old," Monaghan stadium aide John McDevitt told reporters, alluding to extensive corrosion of the steel superstructure. Mayor

Young enthusiastically agreed. "Nobody in their wildest dreams expects that stadium to last beyond ten years," the mayor announced. "Most people say it will fall down in five."[7]

The Fan Club asked the team for a copy of the report—at which point Tiger officials demurred, insisting variously that the study was an "informal" one, or even that no written report existed. Finally, a local newspaper reporter, after nearly a year of Freedom of Information Act requests, uncovered the actual study, at which point the reason for the team's reticence became clear: the consultants, it turned out, had actually recommended only $6 million in renovations—much of it for such items as a new sound system. (The $100 million figure, it turned out, was the price for erecting a dome atop the existing ballpark.) They had never even mentioned any salt damage. The Fan Club—which had initially taken the Tigers' claims at face value—began turning a more discerning eye on the public statements of the team and its political supporters.

So the following March, when the city released a consulting report by stadium-builders Hellmuth Obata Kassebaum—who would stand to make millions off a contract to design and build a new stadium—the Fan Club was prepared for the worst. As expected, HOK's report asserted that a new ballpark was the way to go, estimating that it would cost anywhere from $57 million to $245 million to renovate Tiger Stadium to the point where it would meet the team's needs. Instead, HOK proposed a 56,000-seat stadium with 150 corporate boxes, a helipad, a Domino's Pizza outlet, and no bleacher seats.[8]

By this time, Fan Club members had come to realize that the battle they were engaged in was over far more than merely saving an old ballpark. By the first summer of its operation, the Fan Club newsletter, *Unobstructed Views*, had moved from talking about members' love of Tiger Stadium to asking, "Should public money be used to increase the profits of one of the wealthiest men in the Midwest?...Is the improvement of Mr. Monaghan's

profit margin a more pressing need than the education of our
children, the safety of our senior citizens, the vitality of our
besieged community?"[9] Taking a more political line would cost
the Fan Club some of its original support—two local radio sta-
tions that had sponsored the initial stadium hug backed off
once it was clear the Fan Club meant to take "controversial"
stands—but it also enabled them to draw the links between the
fate of Tiger Stadium and the future of the city as a whole.

Scrambling to counter the renewed push for a new stadium,
the Fan Club struck back in two ways. They launched an
immediate boycott of Domino's Pizza—making more enemies
in a town where Domino's is one of the largest employers.
And they contacted architects John and Judy Davids to prove
that the 800-pound gorilla of the stadium industry was wrong
about renovation.

The Davidses, two young architects from suburban Royal
Oak who drove downtown for dozens of Tiger games every
year, came to the Fan Club late, but they were to become two
of its most important and vocal members. The couple was
already intimately familiar with Tiger Stadium, having
designed a renovated owner's box for Monaghan in the early
'80s. They were also frequent visitors to the ballpark, sitting
sometimes in the owner's box, but more often with their
friends in the right-field bleachers. When the Fan Club called
to ask if they would design a renovation plan for the ballpark,
the Davidses jumped at the chance. Armed with surreptitious-
ly obtained blueprints and the stadium requirements the Tigers
had submitted to HOK, the two spent months of evenings and
weekends laboring over a detailed proposal to provide everything the Tigers had requested without changing the character
of the old ballpark. When completed in January 1990, the
Cochrane Plan (named for an extension to the old ballpark
that would be constructed over seldom-used Cochrane Street,
which ran behind the third-base line) had achieved all its

goals, including expanded concession facilities, club offices, handicapped access, and 73 new luxury boxes. Best of all, the renovation would cost just $26.1 million, a fraction of the price of a new ballpark.[10]

In developing the Cochrane Plan, Fan Club members discovered something else about Tiger Stadium: Not only was it historic, but it also turned out to be one of the most fan-friendly ballparks in the nation. One day in 1989, Frank Rashid was at the Fan Club office when a phone call came in from John Pastier, an architect and student of ballpark history who was looking for information on Tiger Stadium. "Aw, I love Tiger Stadium. With the catwalks!" Rashid recalls Pastier saying. "Not only are you right that it's a great place to watch a ballgame, by *actual mathematical measurement* the average seat at that ballpark is closer [to the field] than the average seat at any other ballpark."

Pastier, a former architecture critic for the *Los Angeles Times*, had the credentials to back up his opinion: His consulting work included contributions to the design of Camden Yards. But his greater passion was seating distances. As part of a project to study the old steel ballparks built in the same era as Tiger Stadium, Pastier had catalogued the average distance from upper-deck seats—the traditional province of the average fan—to home plate in dozens of ballparks across the country. Tiger Stadium, which to fit the most seats in a tightly confined space had been built with the upper deck set atop pillars right above the lower deck, indeed boasted upper-deck seating that was closer to the field than in any other ballpark—barely half the distance as in most of the newer ballparks, including Camden Yards.[11]

The key was in the columns. Anathema to new stadium designers like HOK because they block the view of some fans in the back rows, these steel support beams are absent in every new park built in the last thirty years, necessitating that upper-level seats be cantilevered back from the field in order to support their weight. It's an argument that both Pastier and John Davids dismiss as missing the forest for the girders. In modern ballparks like the new Comiskey, says Davids, "to lose the three or four thousand obstructed seats that they have, they put 20,000 seats twice as far away. Which is a bad tradeoff. If you ask people in Chicago to compare Comiskey, which had columns like Tiger Stadium, to the new Comiskey—they've had real trouble selling their upper-deck tickets. People there were used to sitting close to the field, like Tiger Stadium is. I think once they sat in the upper deck a couple of times, they said, 'We're not going to pay fifteen bucks to sit up here.'"

Though Fan Club members blanched a bit at some items in the Cochrane Plan—particularly the luxury boxes that the Davidses planned to install on the stadium's seldom-used third level, which struck some as an affront to Tiger Stadium's egalitarian spirit—by and large, the plan was applauded as a savvy compromise that would fill the Tigers' needs while saving both public money and the character of the old ballpark.

It also helped convince many Detroiters who might previously have dismissed the Fan Club as a bunch of nostalgic kooks. Bill Dow, a local attorney, first saw the Cochrane Plan scale model on exhibit at the Michigan Gallery, and was so impressed that he immediately joined the Fan Club, quickly becoming a part of the core group. "When I first heard about the [stadium] hug a couple of years earlier, I just kind of thought, 'Aw, boy, what is this?'" he remembers. "But then when I saw the Cochrane Plan I was just so impressed. After meeting with Frank and John Davids and a couple of people down at the Michigan Gallery, the next day I called up and said, 'What can I do to help?'"

The Davidses, flush with praise, proudly called up Tom Monaghan's office to present their plan to their old boss, certain that he would be elated at their work, which would meet every objection of the stadium opponents while saving millions of dollars. "We were telling people at [the Fan Club] meeting, 'No problem, Monaghan's cool,'" Judy Davids later recalled. "We'll just call him, and we'll tell him who we are."[12] Instead, he refused to meet with them. They called Monaghan's home number and spoke to his daughter; according to John Davids, she replied, "Yeah, I mentioned it to him, and he didn't make any commitment to call you."[13]

The Davidses were stunned that their hard work was to be dismissed without even a hearing from the team ownership. Meanwhile, accolades poured in from other corners of Detroit: the *News* and *Free Press* both ran laudatory editorials about the Davidses' proposal, and the city planning commission recommended seriously investigating the renovation option.[14] Pastier says the Cochrane plan would have been "comparable to the Wrigley Field remodeling [in Chicago]—an intelligent, pragmatic way of extending the life of a very important structure, something that was very valuable to the sport in terms of its history and character."

As they lobbied for the Cochrane Plan, the Fan Club continued to fight on other fronts. A committee led by Gruber had successfully lobbied the Department of Interior to place Tiger Stadium on the National Register of Historic Places. The Fan Club mailing list continued to grow, ultimately to 11,000, and hundreds would turn out for periodic demonstrations at the ballpark. (One featured a group of kids pulling toy wagons filled with petitions urging the ballpark be saved.) Their 20 core members, all volunteers, took turns staffing their tiny storefront (donated rent-free by the building's owner, a Fan Club supporter) and standing on the corner of Michigan and Trumbull, where they sold bumper stickers and T-shirts and distributed their newsletter. When Tigers president Bo Schembechler threatened that the team would move if a new stadium were not built, the Fan Club immediately gathered to pore over the team's lease, discovering that it solidly bound the team to play in Detroit until the year 2008, a fact they promptly brought to the media.

Tigers management and their allies, meanwhile, fell back on their original party lines. "I'd rather have the old stadium," Monaghan told reporters in the summer of 1990. "But everybody that knows better wants a new one."[15] The following April, Schembechler, an ex-college football coach who had been hired specifically in the hopes that his iconic status among Michiganders would make him a PR asset, made headlines when he declared in an angry speech before the Economic Club of Detroit, "It's unfair for you to think that you can shackle us to a rusted girder in Tiger Stadium and expect us to compete and win."[16]

That May, Mayor Young again predicted that Tiger Stadium was "about to fall down."[17]

The stadium proponents were starting to run into difficulties selling that story, though, according to John Davids: "The Young administration didn't do a very good job of peddling the idea, and Monaghan's organization was a disaster for that kind of stuff." (Monaghan's nadir came when he inexplicably fired Hall-of-Fame broadcaster Ernie Harwell before the 1991 season, leading to a fan boycott that left thousands of seats vacant on opening day.) But starting in late 1990, Wayne County deputy executive Mike Duggan joined the fray, making the stadium issue a personal crusade. Even as he assured Fan Club representatives that he would seriously consider the Cochrane Plan, Duggan was lobbying hard for a new ballpark, paying special attention to members of the media who had been relatively unreceptive to Monaghan.

County officials "spent an awful lot of money and time taking columnists out to lunch, and making presentations about how many thousands of jobs the stadium would create and how Tiger Stadium was just too old and couldn't be renovated," says

Davids. "They were able to really collar some people and turn some people around who had been supportive of us before."

But though they kept up their rhetoric, the stadium proponents faced a seemingly insurmountable obstacle: There was simply no money to build a new ballpark. The state legislature had rejected repeated attempts to pass stadium-funding bills; Wayne County, meanwhile, was locked in a dispute with the city over where to build a new facility. And when the Detroit city council began mulling putting its own money into the project, the Fan Club led a referendum campaign that resulted, on March 17, 1992, in a resounding 2-1 vote barring any city money from being spent on a new ballpark.

It was, says Rashid, the high-water mark for the Fan Club. Because later that year, two new forces would enter the political mix. Tom Monaghan sold the Tigers for $80 million to Detroit Red Wings owner Mike Ilitch. And Governor John Engler, who had promised on his election in 1990 that no state money would be used to build a new stadium for the Tigers, began searching for a method of doing just that—and a method that would be immune to the desires of the state legislature, or the public.

Act Two: Pizza With Everything

When Mike Ilitch bought the Tigers, Bill Dow remembers, "We thought, here's a chance. This guy's a lifelong Detroiter, he had apparently fond memories of the ballpark. And we thought, here's a chance that maybe we can convince them to buy into renovation of the stadium." Their hopes were buoyed further when Ilitch agreed to meet with them to look over the Cochrane Plan.

Mike Ilitch, like Tom Monaghan, is a pizza baron, his Little Caesar's running neck-and-neck with Domino's for fast-food pizza dominance. More important for the fate of the stadium struggle, he is also a downtown developer whose ties to the city development cabal run deep and strong. He had already been through one sports financing battle in the 1970s when he persuaded the city of Detroit to build a new arena for his Red Wings hockey club. A board member of Detroit Renaissance, the corporate-funded redevelopment organization that dominates city planning, Ilitch spent the better part of the early '90s negotiating the rights to redevelop large swathes of downtown real estate, most notably the historic Fox Theater. He now made use of all of these connections to pressure city political leaders for a new stadium.

Ilitch, explains Dow, was looked on as "a savior of the city—this businessman who put his headquarters downtown. When we met with Senator Carl Levin, he said, 'You know, my daughter would kill me if I didn't fight for renovating Tiger Stadium.' But then he said, 'How do we say no to a guy like Mike Ilitch?'" To further bolster his cause, the pizza king worked behind the scenes with Detroit city officials to grease the political skids for the new park. Over the course of time, two separate city development directors would lobby hard for a new stadium, then leave public office only to turn up on Ilitch's payroll.

Meanwhile, in Lansing, Governor Engler had fixed his attentions on the Governor's Strategic Fund. This was a pool of money that had been set up as a discretionary fund, under the sole control of the governor, to help environmental groups, small businesses, and minority business startups—"kind of a Democratic-inspired slush fund for worthy projects," explains Rashid. Engler had been a staunch opponent of the fund when it was first set up, deriding it as "corporate welfare." Once elected governor, however, he saw it as the perfect vehicle for funding a new Tiger ballpark—so perfect, he announced, that he would augment its modest $20 million in cash reserves with $35 million more from a new tax on casino gambling on Indian reservations that had just been passed by the state legislature.[18]

The Fan Club immediately filed suit against Engler's plan, calling it a blatant misuse of funds and an unconstitutional

end-run around the powers of the state legislature to appropriate money. Every lawyer consulted by the Fan Club remarked
that their suit looked solid—in fact, says Dow, several told the
activists that they had a moral obligation not to allow this
theft of funds to become law. But in its first stop, the circuit
court in Lansing, the case was thrown out, ruling that the gam-
ing moneys were "not state funds."[19] Stunned, the Fan Club
appealed to the state supreme court, which returned a decision
that affirmed the stadium opponents' argument but still ruled
against them: Engler's move was bad law and would not be
allowed to stand as a precedent, but the court would not stand
in the way of *this particular* misappropriation of funds.

Meanwhile, Ilitch's lobbying mechanism had kicked into
high gear. In March 1996, Ilitch and Mayor Dennis Archer
(who was elected to succeed Coleman Young in 1992) went
after the ban on city funding that had been the Fan Club's
greatest victory, staging a public referendum to reverse the
results of the earlier vote. The Fan Club raised about $20,000
to promote the continued ban; the city spent over $600,000.[20]
Archer, remembers Rashid, was on television nearly non-stop
during the weeks leading up to the vote, "every half hour on
the half hour, with glossy fancy ads telling us basically all the
lies, about how the new stadium was going to bring jobs, going
to improve schools and police protection."

Archer also raised for the first time something that had not
been a major issue in the fight over Tiger Stadium: race. The
city politicians behind the stadium push were, like 85 percent
of Detroit, overwhelmingly African-American; the Fan Club
was predominantly white. Organized baseball has long been
one of the worst sports at reaching out to people of color, dat-
ing back to the days of segregated Negro Leagues and continuing to the present day. (One survey found that just 4.8 percent
of fans in attendance at baseball games in 1995 were African-
American, down from 9.8 percent just six years earlier.[21])

Since the Fan Club had made a conscious decision to recruit its membership from Tiger fans, they were left with a membership that was largely, though by no means entirely, white in a majority-minority city.

Archer and his allies in the black political establishment quickly seized upon race as a wedge to drive between the Fan Club and the black electorate. The *Michigan Chronicle*, a local African-American business newspaper, ran a front-page story on Bill Dow headlined "Stadium critic lives in suburbs," the story alluding to "heavy-handed suburban influence" in the upcoming elections. The Fan Club leaders countered that all of its founding members and a majority of its executive committee were from the city, and pointed out that neither Ilitch nor his top aides lived in Detroit. But their arguments fell on deaf ears: "They want us to renovate the old Tiger Stadium, yet when those in the suburbs build, they build new," wrote V. Lonnie Peek in a *Chronicle* op-ed. "Detroit deserves a new stadium, not a renovated old one."[22]

The city funding ban fell by a more than 4-1 margin. Soon afterward, the Detroit Lions announced that they, too, would be moving back downtown to play in a separate football stadium to be built at public expense. The total cost in public dollars: an estimated $240 million.

Epilogue: Monoculture

"Here is a tremendous theater," Frank Rashid says, pointing to a parking lot. He is driving through downtown Detroit, or what's left of it. "This was the Michigan Theater—wonderful lobby. It's all gone." Down the street a ways sits the Fox Theater, recently renovated by Mike Ilitch after city development director Emmet Moten arranged to have it condemned and sold to Ilitch at a $2 million loss to the city.[23] Across the street from the Fox is the United Artists, which Ilitch similarly arranged to have the city transfer to his control, and which the pizza king may now tear down to provide additional parking for the two new stadiums.

Perhaps more than any other modern American city, Detroit has in recent decades pursued a "development" strategy that seems destined to transform its entire downtown into vacant lots. It began in the 1950s with the construction of five major downtown freeways—"they cut through the city, cut it to ribbons," says Rashid, who remembers, as a college student camped out outside Tiger Stadium for World Series tickets in 1968, watching the Fisher Freeway plow through the neighboring Briggs Community. Detroit's old city hall fell soon after, to be replaced by a sterile plaza dubbed Cadillac Square. The city's classic Orchestra Hall was almost replaced by a McDonald's several years ago, before a concerted public campaign brought it back from the brink; meanwhile, the city's oldest brick residential building was bought by entertainer Anita Baker, and torn down to make way for an International House of Pancakes.

In their place, downtown Detroit is littered with the remains of failed redevelopment schemes. As Rashid's battered Subaru approaches the city center, a tiny electric train car breezes by atop a concrete track that winds in a tight loop through downtown Detroit. This is the "people-mover," an ill-fated light-rail scheme that cost millions of dollars in federal funds for a mass transit system that goes nowhere, and is seldom used.

"What I'm going to do now is take you down Woodward," says Rashid, "so you can see what happened to the city's main street." He pulls the car south onto Woodward Avenue, and into a scene of utter devastation. Detroit's downtown shopping district is simply gone. Cavernous department stores and jewelry outlets, blocks and blocks of them, sit vacant and shuttered. In the 1980s, the giant Hudson's department store—the Macy's of Detroit—fled to a suburban mall, and its neighbors along Woodward quickly followed. Now only the buildings remain, and these not for long: The city has announced plans to demolish the Hudson's building, empty since the early '80s, and the others may soon follow.

The car turns off Woodward and bears east along the Detroit River, and suddenly there looms the centerpiece of Detroit's failed hopes: the Renaissance Center, four gleaming steel-and-glass towers isolated from the rest of the city by giant ivy-coated concrete berms. Henry Ford II, grandson of the company's founder, raised the money for the center in the '70s—"maybe he realized that the Ford Motor Company hadn't built a car in Detroit since 1914 and felt guilty about what had happened in Detroit," says Rashid. Ford had offered to build several smaller developments scattered around downtown, but Mayor Young's predecessor, Roman Gribbs, instead chose a megalith that utterly transformed downtown, all right, but not quite in the way that was intended. "All those great buildings downtown that had high office occupancy, [their tenants have] moved to this place and now they're empty," says Rashid. "[The city] basically moved downtown over by a quarter of a mile, and contributed to the devastation of Woodward."

Rashid steers past Cobo Arena, the Pistons' waterfront arena until they moved to the suburbs in the '80s; and the adjoining Joe Louis Arena, built with $26 million in city funds for Ilitch's Red Wings in 1979. "And now Ilitch wants another hockey arena, because he doesn't like Joe Louis [Arena]," says Rashid.

"We say in Detroit that we have a lousy class of rich people," he muses. "They dumped on the city, they abused it, they exploited it, they controlled it, and then they left it." Until the 1920s, Detroit's economy boasted a variety of small manufacturing industries. The rise of the auto industry put an end to that, says Rashid, creating an economy of booms and busts and continuous plant closings and reopenings, and a largely Southern-born labor force that erupted in racial antagonism each time the industry took a downturn. The Ford Motor Company, in particular, hopped from Detroit to suburban

Highland Park to neighboring River Rouge, leaving crumbling factories and displaced lives in its wake. "Each time," according to Rashid, "[Henry Ford] built up a labor force, a tax base, and then abandoned it, and then foisted off the social costs of his erratic business, his layoffs, and all of that on the cities. It's a fascinating story of abuse of the public coffers."

In the 1980s, General Motors, another auto giant that had fled to the suburbs, agreed to return to downtown Detroit—in exchange for the city's agreement to demolish Poletown, a thriving if poor neighborhood of 10,000, to make way for a sprawling auto plant. Now there is talk that GM regards the Poletown plant as obsolete, and is looking to move out of town again.

Rashid drives back through downtown, finally stopping the car in a wasteland of empty lots behind the Fox Theater. This, he explains, is the site projected for parking for Ilitch's new baseball stadium. The city, through its powers of eminent domain, is in the process of seizing this spacious property from its private owners who use it as parking lots, and handing it over to Ilitch at cost—to use as parking lots.

Ilitch and his supporters like to boast that the Tigers' owner hasn't demanded the total subsidies that other teams have extorted from their hometowns. The Tigers' 1997 program, for example, after a page of tributes to the old stadium that are largely lifted from Fan Club materials, notes that "it became clear that a new facility was needed to replace the aging and venerable park," and that the new stadium's financing "will include $145 million from the Tigers, the highest team-based financing for a Major League Baseball facility since the Dodgers built Dodger Stadium in 1962." But like Dodger Stadium, which was built with private money on a gift of huge swathes of valuable public land, Ilitch's contribution comes with its own hidden subsidy: the Fan Club projects that *all* of this "team-based" money will be covered by revenues from the city-donated parking lots.

It's a pattern that is all too familiar to lifelong Detroiters like Rashid. "One of the things that the auto companies did was make us hungry for the single interest," he says, surveying the wreckage of his city's downtown. "We're so used to being a single-industry town—it's too bad that our single industry is now pizza. Pizza and entertainment—it's now Mike Ilitch. We have ceded over to him one-sixth of downtown."

It is the opening of another baseball season, the 86th for Tiger Stadium, the 102nd at the corner of Michigan and Trumbull. But Rashid and the remaining core members of the Fan Club—Kim Stroud, the Davidses, Bill Dow, Catherine Darin—no longer spend their days down in the Tiger Stadium bleachers that they lobbied to save. Press reports had already disclosed that Ilitch had been using the 90-cent city ticket tax, earmarked for maintenance of Tiger Stadium once the 1970s renovations were complete, for such items as pizza pans at the Little Caesar's concessions stands at the stadium's new food court. Now, in the bitterest irony of all, the city has decreed that Ilitch will be allowed to use the surcharge to pay for the *demolition* of the old ballpark. Frank Rashid, who devoted ten years of his life to saving Tiger Stadium, cannot even go and say goodbye without helping finance its destruction.

What began as a whim by five baseball-loving friends bloomed into a movement that held off the city's political and corporate leadership for almost a decade. And yet in the end they lost their war. "We did everything we could do, legally and politically," says Rashid, with more than a touch of sadness. "We used the system. We tried to believe in the system. I don't believe in the system any more. I mean, I didn't really believe in it before, but I thought, well, give it a chance to work. But it clearly doesn't work. If you don't have money and power, the system will not work for you—that's one thing I've learned."

6 HOME FIELD ADVANTAGE

"For most of us, we feel that supply and demand, the market, capitalism has got us where we are today in the United States, and so there ought to be some sense, some obligation, to allow that to continue."
—RANDY JOHNSON, PRESIDENT,
ORLANDO AREA SPORTS COMMISSION

"This is not about a very rich guy born with a spoon in his mouth that is trying to add to his riches and got the community to build something for him. This is the community saying—in the form of all the major companies—'This is good for the community, let's go forward with this.'"
—JERRY COLANGELO, OWNER OF THE
PHOENIX SUNS AND ARIZONA DIAMONDBACKS[1]

Detroit may offer a dramatic example, but it's hardly alone. In most cities, stadium deals are less an exception to standard urban policy than part of the everyday wheeling and dealing that goes on for public money. The question, then, is if corporate welfare, whether for sports teams or auto plants, is so obviously unprofitable for local governments, why keep shelling out the dough?

After ten years of watching Detroit politicians fight for a new baseball stadium, the self-interest of elected officials in giant giveaways certainly seems obvious to Frank Rashid. "The local politicians, particularly the mayor and the county executive, know that they get far more mileage out of having a big new project than out of a renovation," he explains. "They have the ability to say who gets the contracts, whose land is used, which developers are employed, which bond attorneys do it—and all of those people are the people who contribute to their campaign war chest." That, he believes, is why expensive projects like new stadiums win out over small-scale ones like the Tiger Stadium Fan Club's Cochrane Plan: "Not because they are intrinsically better for the city, or better for the team or anything. There is a political interest in doing it."

This tendency has only worsened as local economies have become more dependent on footloose corporations for their economic well-being, says corporate welfare researcher Greg LeRoy. "The Fortune 500 is still killing off 1,000 to 2,500 full-time jobs a day, so it's easy for companies to get governors and mayors to compete for the few remaining good projects that are happening," he observes. "And now it's really an expectation of a company, if you're going to relocate or construct a major new facility, you'd probably lose your job as CFO of that company if you didn't go shake a state down for eight figures. It's just part of your job description now."

If there is anyone who resists these deals, interestingly, it's usually state legislatures and city councils, which reap less of the publicity benefits and are left with the task of filling the resulting budget shortfalls. Says LeRoy, "There's a lot of very skeptical state legislatures that have been trying to rein in their governors and city councils that have been trying to rein in their mayors—it really is an executive/legislative tension. You see that theme over and over again."

As for sports team owners, they can count not only on their lure as economic investors (albeit a rather small one, proportionally), but on the popularity of their product, which can't be matched by any mere car company. Politicians already predisposed to salivating at the prospect of announcing a new "job-creation" deal can get absolutely fanatical when the deal involves their favorite teams. Minnesota Governor Arne Carlson, a key backer of new sports facilities in his state, has said he wants to be a college sports booster when he retires from politics. Cleveland Mayor Michael White spent months talking of little but the Browns to local media during the fight over that team. And in an exceptional display of sports exuberance, San Francisco Mayor Willie Brown declared that he would "do 100 [campaign] appearances in a week if I had to" in campaigning for a new stadium for the 49ers, and whooped and hollered for several minutes when the favorable referendum results came in.[2] "He wasn't close to hysterical," said the radio reporter who watched as Brown, a 49ers cap on his head, climbed onto a table and swilled champagne from the bottle, screaming at the top of his lungs. "He was hysterical."[3]

The free tickets that are commonly distributed to local political leaders no doubt help grease these political wheels. But the most crucial asset for sports owners is the likelihood of a legislative body for whom a sports star like Jerry Rice, or even a high-powered owner like Edward Bennett Williams, is a celebrity of the first order. As Daniel Finley, county executive of Wisconsin's Waukesha County, told the Sports Facilities Finance conference, "You send Robin Yount or Hank Aaron into the state capital, and they melt."

Add in the generally chummy relationship between politicians and local business leaders, and you have a scenario ripe for exploitation. "It's incredibly incestuous," says Ricky Rask, a child-care activist in Minneapolis who has become a leader in that city's fight against public spending on a new ballpark.

"Everybody's got a finger in here or a finger in there. They all play golf together." Fears of losing out to other cities, Rask is convinced, are just a smokescreen for politicians whose ties to the old boys network are so strong that they are eager to provide for their friends, even at the cost of hundreds of millions of dollars to the public treasury.

Paying to Win

Fortunately for the residents of cities run by these subsidy-happy politicians, local democracy has another means of controlling the public purse: referenda, through which voters can override the will of their elected officials at the ballot box. Not as fortunately, the electoral process has proven to be as susceptible to the power of big money as the politicians themselves.

The opposition to stadium-funding referenda has taken many forms in different cities, from established anti-tax or economic-justice groups to ad-hoc groups of individual citizens. But in every case, they have one commonality: None of them has even a fraction of the money of the stadium proponents. "It was beyond David vs. Goliath," moaned Campaign to Stop the Giveaway organizer Jim Ross to San Francisco reporters, after his campaign against public funding for the 49ers' new stadium was outspent 20-1 by stadium backers. "David at least had a sling. We were throwing rocks with our hands."[4]

A rare glimpse behind the scenes of a pro-stadium campaign was provided at the 1997 Sports Facilities Finance conference, when Jay Cross, president of the Miami Heat basketball team, transfixed listeners with his team's tale of extracting a new sports arena from their county government. By the fall of 1996, the Miami Heat had spent their entire eight-year existence at the Miami Arena, a combined hockey-basketball facility that Dade County had spent $53 million to construct in 1988. Unfortunately for the county, that was the exact moment when the economics of basketball underwent a seismic shift: The National Basketball Association was soaring in popularity, and luxury suites were just taking off as a major money-maker. Miami Arena, with its paltry 16 suites and 15,000-seat capacity, instantly found itself on the small end of league facilities. As stadium consultant Marc Ganis described it, "That facility was obsolete—economically obsolete—before the concrete dried."

The Florida Panthers hockey club, which had shared the Miami Arena with the Heat since the team's founding in 1993, had already whipsawed Dade County and neighboring Broward County into a bidding war for its services, a battle ultimately won by Broward with a winning bid of $212 million. Heat owner Mickey Arison, the billionaire owner of Carnival Cruise Lines, followed with his own demands, proposing first $60 million in renovations to the still-new arena, then a whole new building of his own. By leveraging the threat to join the Panthers in Broward County, Arison ultimately arrived at an agreement for a $162.5 million arena on the Miami waterfront, of which Dade County would pay three-quarters, the team the rest.

The Miami populace, however, was somewhat less obliging. A local lawyer—"an annoying little man," as Cross would describe him to his listeners at the Grand Hyatt—gathered 48,000 signatures to put the arena deal on the November ballot. The election was just eight weeks away. Polls were running 60-40 against the publicly funded arena, and the leading candidate for Dade County mayor was a vocal opponent. Cross, sensing impending disaster, came to a decision. "This is a political campaign," he recalled thinking. "This is no different than if you're running for the Senate, or governor, or mayor. We're talking about winning the hearts and minds of the voters."

To that end, Cross brought in Mike Murphy of Murphy Pintak Gaulter, the firm that had managed the successful gubernatorial campaigns of such GOP standouts as New Jersey's Christine Todd Whitman, Wisconsin's Tommy Thompson, and Michigan's John Engler.[5] The first thing

Murphy told the team, according to Cross, was to "get ready to spend some serious coin." A typical mayoral campaign will cost around $2 million over the course of a year; the Coalition for a Greater Miami—the political action committee formed by the team to run the pro-arena campaign—would ultimately spend an astonishing $3.7 million in just eight weeks to convince Dade County voters of the rightness of their cause.

"The next thing we found out from our polls," continued Cross, "was that Pat Riley's one of the most popular guys around." Riley, the longtime NBA coach (and motivational book author) whose contract with the Heat gave him part-ownership of the team, became the centerpiece of the hundreds of TV commercials that all those millions of PAC dollars were buying, with an escalating series of messages (in both English and Spanish) designed to peak in the days right before the election. In the earliest commercials, a smiling, shirtsleeved Riley, a basketball under his arm, cajoled viewers with promises of "a fantastic waterfront park, a safe, fun place for families to enjoy, with shops, restaurants, and a championship arena," as a computer-generated flyby of the new arena filled the screen.

By the week before the election, the televised images had changed. The message now "went negative," explained Cross. Riley's friendly appeal was gone; in its place, images of vacant lots and a voiceover that intoned, "This is the waterfront the politicians want to save. Broken concrete. A haven for criminals. Dade County deserves better: a safe new waterfront park for all our families. Existing tourist taxes pay the bill, so you don't have to. But some politicians want to kill the new waterfront park, and keep the tourist money for their wasteful spending." Although Cross says proudly that the team never directly threatened to leave town if the arena weren't built, the possibility became a less than subtle theme of the ads as well, as residents were depicted reciting the campaign's new slogan: "Vote No, so the Heat won't go."

The arena campaign, as befitting the money and expertise brought to it, was slick, subtle, and convincing. By the week before the vote, the Heat had wooed the support of the mayor as well. ("He realized that driving the local millionaire out of town is not exactly smart politics," bragged Cross.)

The final vote was 59 percent to 41 percent, in favor of the Heat. For $3.7 million, the basketball team had bought a 19 percentage point swing in the polls.

Corporate Cheerleaders

The Heat's successful manipulation of public opinion points up the difficulty of pinning down "public sentiment" on corporate welfare—it all depends on how you ask the question, and those intent on manipulating the process will always ask the question in the way that will most benefit their interests. "The public" doesn't, by and large, see the behind-the-scenes maneuvering that Cross described. For most people, the story consists of what appears on TV and in the print media—and that picture often bears little resemblance to reality.

The media are seldom credited as key boosters of stadium deals, if only because for the owners and their allies, they can seem like an enemy of their PR attempts, uncovering uncomfortable details of the deal going down. Certainly, much stadium reporting is negative—with all the dirty facts of stadium deals, even a lazy reporter can't help but stumble over a few by accident.

Yet a few incisive articles do little to change the *premises* on which the stadium debate is reported, which often seem lifted straight from the teams' PR manuals. As media critics point out, a few critical articles can easily coexist with a greater editorial push in favor of a project. "There are so many self-deluded reporters in the mainstream media who sneak the truth into one story out of every 20 they write and think they've done their job, because the truth got out," observes Jim Naureckas, editor of the media-watch magazine *Extra!* But the impact of news, he notes, is in its repetition, and occasionally showing glimpses of one side of the story can serve to strengthen the apparent "objectivity" of press coverage that is in fact skewed mightily in one direction.

What's more important than isolated articles, as far as public sentiment is concerned, is how the media frame the issue. Even when critical of some fine point of a deal, they seldom question the need for a new stadium, invariably editorializing against legislators who "hunker down behind the public opinion polls."[6] In this context, public opposition is presented as a mere temporary obstacle to the inevitable course of progress, which will ultimately—*should* ultimately—result in a new sports facility being built.

In Seattle, for example, after voters had narrowly defeated a proposal to build a new stadium for the Mariners baseball team in September 1995, *The Seattle Times*—which had provided free ad space for the pro-stadium campaign—first editorialized that this represented "a striking affirmation of the region's commitment to baseball...half of King County voters would tax themselves to keep the team there." (That slightly over half had voted *not* to tax themselves wasn't deemed worthy of notice.) The next day, the paper ran a front-page story headlined "Stadium Not Yet Dead," in which it suggested ways that the state government could go ahead with the stadium despite the popular vote.[7] One month later, the state legislature would do just that.

This type of coverage, in which the stadium campaign is itself portrayed almost as a sporting event where the paper roots along with the home team, is endemic to stadium coverage. "49ers drive toward goal as clock ticks down," read one *San Francisco Examiner* headline two days before the public vote on that team's new football stadium.[8] In this "pennant-race" coverage, stories become more focused on who's winning or losing than in digging out the truthfulness of the two sides' arguments. The day before the 49ers referendum, a *San Francisco Chronicle* columnist led off his column on a debate between San Francisco Mayor Willie Brown and California state senator Quentin Kopp over the new 49ers stadium by writing that Brown had "won on points," beneath the headline "Brown Wins With His Jabbing."[9] It was left to the readers' imagination whether the debate had revealed anything of substance.

"Who Are You Guys?"

As with elected officials, there's no shortage of possible reasons why the media are so owner-friendly.

The most straightforward theory was summarized by Beth Hawkins of the *Minneapolis City Pages* in her analysis of that city's media coverage of stadium deals: "Sports editors and writers freely acknowledge the symbiosis that exists between the news media and pro sports. Newspapers create excitement among fans, who drive up ticket sales. And while pro teams themselves don't create a lot of advertising, a thriving franchise attracts readers to the paper who might not otherwise pick it up."[10] In Seattle, Hawkins reported, press runs of newspapers the day after a game are increased by anywhere from ten to 20 percent, depending on which team played and whether it won or lost.

But newspapers, especially newspaper *owners*, have a greater stake in stadiums and other development projects than mere sales figures. Modern media enterprises are major corporations themselves, whose publishers often share team owners' interests in promoting public subsidies of business interests and downtown development. In many cities, including Cleveland, Seattle, Milwaukee, and Minneapolis, local newspaper publishers have helped fund pro-stadium lobbying efforts, or even registered as lobbyists themselves to press legislators on their hometown team's behalf.

The most egregious example of media self-interest may be the *Minneapolis Star Tribune*, whose then-publisher, John Cowles Jr., raised $10.5 million to help city officials buy land for the Metrodome in the late '70s—in exchange for the right to develop some 200 acres of land surrounding the site. (*Star Tribune* staffers later took out a full-page ad disassociating themselves from the paper's Metrodome coverage.) Following Cowles' death in 1983, his successors at Cowles Media continued to carry the flame for the Twins' stadium dreams, making unspecified donations to the team's lobbying arm. The donations are well worth the gamble: If a new stadium is built, the paper will stand to cash in on the parking lots that would rise on the downtown property that it acquired in the Metrodome deal.[11]

Media self-interest in sports is only likely to increase as media owners increasingly *become* sports owners. If Rupert Murdoch's News Corp. succeeds in buying the Los Angeles Dodgers, five teams—the Atlanta Braves, Atlanta Hawks, Anaheim Angels, Mighty Ducks of Anaheim, and the Dodgers—will be controlled by three of the largest media conglomerates in the U.S.: Disney, News Corp., and Time-Warner. The *Chicago Tribune* owns both the Cubs and their broadcast outlet, WGN. Even local media outlets have begun getting in on the deal: The new Arizona Diamondbacks baseball team is part-owned by the *Arizona Republic* newspaper, putting its publisher in business with Jerry Colangelo, the owner of three of Phoenix's four major-league sports teams.

Media owners are quick to deny that these interlocking business deals represent a conflict of interest. They claim that their papers maintain an impenetrable wall between reporters and management, and furthermore point to the critical stories they have published on stadium projects (often alongside pro-stadium editorials). *The Seattle Times* went so far as to point to its coverage of its own gift of free ads to the Mariners' pro-stadium campaign as a sign of its impartiality: That story, asserted executive editor Michael Francher in an editorial, never "would have been published in a newspaper whose reporting is affected by the publisher of the editorial page."[12]

But far from an impenetrable wall, the experience of numerous reporters has been that the division between management and editorial is more like a thin screen, across which publishers can subtly influence news coverage while staying technically out of sight. One of the most insightful looks into the inner workings of journalistic self-censorship is *Fear and Favor in the Newsroom*, an hour-long documentary produced by California Newsreel. In it, the filmmakers compiled the stories of various reporters who were forced out of their jobs when their zeal for journalism grew stronger than their willingness to toe the corporate line. An award-winning consumer reporter is accused of "bias" for correctly predicting that a nuclear power plant was driving its parent company into bankruptcy. A veteran newsman is fired by NBC for trying to report on Iraqi civilian casualties of U.S. bombing during the Gulf War. In story after story, journalists told how despite claims of a hands-off policy, on "controversial" issues, management can easily make its wishes known—and carried out.

60 Minutes producer Lowell Bergman, for example, while insisting that he has been able to get unpleasant truths across on his program, told the filmmakers, "It's never been as heavyhanded as someone saying, 'You can't do that story.' But I think it's understood that when you get into that area that you are in a dangerous area."

Sydney Schanberg, the Pulitzer Prize–winning journalist, had his *New York Times* career ended when he stepped on one too many toes. "It happens sort of by osmosis," he explained in the documentary. "There are no notes posted on the bulletin board. Senior editors usually do not tell desk editors like the city editor, 'We don't want you to cover this, we want you to cover that instead.'" Nonetheless, Schanberg found out the hard way that there are lines not to be crossed; when he used his column to criticize the *Times* and other local papers for focusing on soft news like restaurant openings rather than exposing government wrongdoing, he was shoved out the door.

Schanberg's mistake, according to his former colleague John Hess, was in trying to cover New York City in the same way he would Cambodia. "The paper finds it really hard," Hess told the filmmakers, "to tolerate this kind of hard, controversial journalism about the people the publisher is eating with every day." Although the desired slant is seldom phrased in terms of pleasing corporate sponsors, that is still the hidden message, explained Wendell Rawls Jr., an *Atlanta Constitution* staffer who quit when a popular muckraking editor was forced out in favor of a new chief brought in from *USA Today*. "This attitude pervades the entire newspaper, that we are trying to make people feel better about themselves somehow, rather than letting them hold up a mirror to themselves."[13]

Perhaps it's this kind of unstated pressure that produces in journalists what Frank Rashid of the Tiger Stadium Fan Club calls "studied incompetence." New reporters coming onto the stadium beat, he says, seemed ignorant even of their own newspaper's previous coverage of the story. "You'd think at least that person would have the intelligence, especially in this computer age, to go back and check the stories that had been written before. I don't think that *ever* happens. We were having to reorient reporters into the story consistently."

On one occasion, Rashid recalls, he wound up calling the *Free Press* to complain about an inaccurate story about the Fan Club. He pointed out to a city desk editor that the reporter had printed inaccurate statements by the group's opponents about the Fan Club, statements that the reporter himself had to have known were untrue.

The editor, according to Rashid, replied with indignation, "What do you expect? Monaghan has made money. He's paid his dues. Who are you guys?"

"I really appreciated the honesty," says Rashid. "But, damn! None of us is disreputable. We're all people who are solid citizens, but we don't have money. Solid citizens without money don't count as well as somebody who's got a big corporation. So it doesn't matter that we worked for several years on the issue, or established a track record of being credible, or anything like that."

The Usual Suspects

Finally, no picture of the urban power structure would be complete without the group that *The Seattle Times* referred to as "The Civic Power Brokers No One Elected."[14] They are the bond lawyers who are called in to give legal authorization for deals between cities and banks when major bond issues are involved, and they are part of the massive network of profit-makers that has been making money off of urban debt—especially major deals like new stadiums—for decades.

In Seattle, the law firm of Preston, Gates & Ellis stands to make a cool $145,000 for its role as legal counsel in the City Council's authorization of $336 million in bonds to pay for a new home for the Seattle Mariners. The firm, "the king of bondsmakers in Washington State," according to the *Times*, handled 60 percent of the state's bond work in 1996.[15]

It is up to their attorneys to declare bonds legally enforceable. If they do, and the bond issue is approved, they collect a fee, sometimes topping $1 million. The role that bond lawyers play in encouraging municipalities to go into debt over massive construction projects may be largely behind-the-scenes, but it's hardly a secret. "These guys take council members and 'educate' them about finances. 'Here's a nice building that you can be remembered by,'" Jordan Brower, a Seattle activist, told *The Seattle Times*.[16]

How influential are bond lawyers and the huge firms they represent? The recent Sports Facilities Finance conference in New York was officially the "Municipal Issuers' & Sports Franchises' Symposium on Sports Facilities Finance"—note the "issuers." Hobnobbing amongst the representatives of professional sports teams and urban governments were lawyers and representatives of some of the country's biggest Wall Street law firms. The convention wouldn't have happened without them.

One Dollar, One Vote

For owners and their political allies, money provides a way around not just the media but the public as well. Having learned from the experiences of franchises like the Heat, teams will seldom go into a public vote without a multimillion-dollar budget for TV commercials and other PR strategies. The biggest spender of all: Microsoft co-founder Paul Allen, who, in a rush to get a football-stadium referendum on the Washington state ballot before his option to buy the Seattle Seahawks expired, simply offered the state $4.2 million to avoid the time-consuming signature-gathering phase usually required to put a proposal on the state ballot. The state legislature happily took him up on the offer, and Allen went on to spend another $5 million (in six weeks) on lobbying the public for a positive vote.[16]

When Minnesota's Metropolitan Sports Facility Commission began hearings on publicly funding a new stadium, says activist Ricky Rask, they were careful to exclude the public in every way possible, shifting meeting dates at the last minute and denying time for public comment. The third or fourth time Rask showed up at a "public hearing" and was denied time to speak, she says, "I stood up and I said, 'Excuse me, but if you're not going to allow public testimony, then you need to retract this statement. Do one or the other, but make it clear about what you're going to do.'" The commissioners tried to silence Rask—"Oh, gee, they were mad!" she recalls—but with TV news cameras on the scene (at Rask's invitation), they had little choice but to open the meetings to public testimony.

Frank Rashid and Kim Stroud had a similar experience at the Wayne County hearings on allocating public money for a new stadium for the Tigers. "It was supposed to be a public hearing," Rashid says. "We heard about it a day before. Kim called up and said what time is the hearing, and they said it begins at noon. We stayed up all night, worked on materials— we knew that they were going to approve it, but we thought we had at least to go down there."

When the Fan Club activists arrived at the county building, they were told that the hearing had in fact started at 9 a.m., though it was continuing through the afternoon. Rashid put his name down to speak, and they settled in to wait for the public comment section. "Finally we got an agenda for the afternoon session, and there was a vote scheduled—and *after* the vote, there was public comment." Only one "member of the public" did get to speak before the vote, he notes wryly: Denise Ilitch Lites, Tiger owner Mike Ilitch's daughter.

The Carrot and the Stick

There are cities, of course, where the coalition doesn't fall neatly together, where a stubborn politician, or a particularly skeptical press, stops a deal for the time being. But mayors and editors come and go, while businessmen such as sports owners stay on—and if the wait is too long for an impatient owner, he can always sell at a profit to someone else who will play the stadium game in his place.

Moreover, for stadiums as for other corporate subsidies, the burden is on the local government once the deal is in place. If it fails to live up to its end of the bargain, the corporation can simply take its business elsewhere; but a corporation that fails to come through with the jobs or economic development it promised a locality can simply shrug its shoulders and blame the vagaries of the economy—assuming anyone ever even thinks to ask.

Over the past few years, cities and states have begun exploring methods of holding corporations to their end of the bargain, specifically through "clawback" legislation that would force companies to repay their subsidies if job or economic goals are not met within a specified time. But as these depend on enforcement by the same public officials who approve the deals in the first place, corporations are seldom if ever held accountable for their actions.

Arthur Rolnick, a vice president at the Minneapolis Federal Reserve who has campaigned for years against "the economic war among the states," can't see local politicians ever putting an end to corporate welfare. "In some sense, they come out of it a hero," he says. "The businesses that are involved with this thing, they love this deal, they're getting big benefits, and you can bet that they're going to support this guy's campaign. For the public, they're against it, maybe, but it's one of many issues, and when it comes time to vote, there's a million other issues, and this thing's probably already been done, and so they move on. So it looks like, the way the political aspects of it work, there isn't much downside for these guys."

The downside for the public, though, is another story. Often several stories, in fact, as different interests fight to prevent the brunt of the corporate welfare burden from falling on them. Nowhere were these competing interests more evident than in the case of baseball's oldest stadium, which became one of its earliest stadium battles: Chicago's Comiskey Park.

7 LOCAL HEROES

"If you have to survive, you don't have time to get discouraged."
—WENTWORTH GARDENS COMMUNITY
ACTIVIST HALLIE AMEY

John Aranza has always been somewhat leery of radicals who make a lot of sound and fury for their various causes. His own community activism was centered on electoral politics, his church, the Boys and Girls Clubs—until the Chicago White Sox demanded a replacement for 80-year-old Comiskey Park, then threatened to leave town, and his life was changed forever.

The White Sox threatening to leave might not have changed Hallie Amey's life all that much, if the team hadn't ended up putting her neighbors' homes in the bulldozer's path. When it became clear that the community she had called home for decades was in jeopardy, the spirited senior citizen decided to do something about it. But then again, Amey has been a community activist for just about her whole life. More than forty years a resident in Wentworth Gardens, a small Chicago housing project on the city's south side, Amey long ago learned that if you wanted to get something done, you have to do it yourself.

It was early spring 1986, and one of baseball's most storied franchises was about to set in motion an unlikely chain of events that would see a historic landmark gutted, dozens of homes and businesses torn to the ground, a new trend in stadium architecture and a newly dominant architectural firm emerge, and, perhaps most unexpectedly, a remarkable convergence occur in the lives of John Aranza, Hallie Amey, and so many more.

Warning Bells

By the mid-1980s, the relatively new owners of the White Sox had escalated their rumblings of dissatisfaction with 75-year-old Comiskey Park and its urban neighborhood. When Jerry Reinsdorf and Edward M. Einhorn purchased the team from Bill Veeck in 1981, it didn't take long for them to decide they wanted more—more television revenues, more attendance at games, more profit from the franchise. Their complaints about the state of the old stadium, the safety of its neighborhood, and their ability to turn a profit grew louder, as did their flirtation with St. Petersburg, Florida, to move their team to that region.[1]

Local fans began to get alarmed. "We were afraid to speak up then," says Aranza. "I'm no activist, but I'll tell you what I did. It's the first time I ever did this in my life."

Aranza grew up on the South Side of Chicago, home to the city's famous meatpacking industry, century-old Irish neighborhoods, monstrous housing projects, and many of its most infamous politicians. He and his wife make their home in Bridgeport—a white ethnic Chicago neighborhood (one of the city's oldest) known for producing, among other things, future mayors of the city. On Memorial Day 1986, the Aranzas had relatives over for a barbecue on their back patio. From their small bungalow, John could see the light towers of Comiskey Park, and the team's uncertain future was very much on his mind. Aranza remembers the day when, standing there at the family barbecue, he realized he'd had enough. The White Sox were going to move, he told his wife. "You know what?" he remembers saying. "I got a feeling they're gonna move the ball-club. They're going to tear down the ballpark. It's terrible, I don't know what to do."

Aranza asked his wife to get him something he could make a sign with. She returned with an old pillowcase, on which he composed a homemade sign, "Save Our Sox."

With two pieces of bamboo holding up the pillowcase, Aranza made his way the few blocks to Comiskey Park, where he stood on the curb with his homemade sign. When passers-by questioned him, Aranza could only reply, "I've got a feeling the ballpark's going to be torn down." Some folks ignored him, others asked what they could do. "'I don't know,' I said. 'Write your congressman. Write the owners. Write state legislators,' I says, 'I don't know who. Write local TV people. Just something.'" After some time the bamboo broke, and Aranza just held his sign in his hands. "I must have looked like somebody on a desert island, waiting for a passing ship to see it, to rescue me, to rescue the ballpark," he says. "I never did this in my life. Never in my life."

His one-man demonstration might have been the end of it, but for similar concerns that were plaguing Mary O'Connell, a lifelong White Sox fan despite living on the city's North Side. (Chicago has many historically deep divides between its geographic North and South Sides—the North largely being home to the city's elegant tree-lined streets and upper-class white residents and the South the traditional manufacturing base and home to the town's ethnic white working-class and black populations. The city's baseball fans are as deeply split, with the National League Cubs making their home, and taking their fan base from, the North Side, and the White Sox firmly a South Side team.)

"I saw an article in one of the Chicago papers talking about how the White Sox needed a new stadium," O'Connell says.

She was surprised at the paper's easy acceptance that Comiskey Park had supposedly outlived its useful life.

Alarmed, O'Connell wrote to the team management and received a cursory response, referring to an enclosed one-paragraph engineering report. She compares the terse justification for tearing down the old stadium to a decision to condemn a house because the roof leaked. "Wouldn't you expect that there would be some kind of analysis or numbers, some kind of detailed description about the state of the girders or the concrete or the wiring or the masonry, or something that would say, 'Well, here's this problem, and in order to repair that it would cost this much money'?" O'Connell found herself wondering. "But it was nothing, it was just this one little one-paragraph thing."

O'Connell responded with an op-ed piece in the *Chicago Sun-Times*. It was after the piece ran that an acquaintance suggest she get in touch with John Aranza.

Saving the Team

"Now when Mary called me," Aranza says, "she said, 'John, we're starting this group and I really want you to be a part of it.' And I didn't want to be. I never did anything, I stayed away from activism and groups, however you want to call it, my entire life, only because none ever appealed to me.

"She would beg me on the phone and I said, 'No, but good luck to you,' and she kept calling me, so I agreed to go to one of the meetings that she had proposed, and it was out of that the Save Our Sox was formed."

The group's initial focus was on keeping the team in the city and preventing the destruction of Comiskey Park. "Our argument was why rip down one of these [old stadiums] and build a brand-new monstrosity that nobody would want to go and see," says O'Connell. "Why not play up the fact that you've got these two great old ballparks? Use that to attract people and get people to come." If anything, O'Connell and her colleagues argued, public money could be used to preserve and maintain the site's history and appeal. To that end, they campaigned to have the old stadium declared a national monument, to be run by the National Park Service. "If you're going to use tax dollars," says O'Connell, "let's build up the charm and intimacy of the historic ballpark that we have."

Nicknamed the "Baseball Palace of the World" in its heyday, Comiskey Park's fan-friendly construction (both decks of seating stretched to the playing field, putting spectators right up against the action) and colorful history (Shoeless Joe Jackson and the scandalous Black Sox of 1919 played there, along with the 1959 pennant-winning team) made it a proud city landmark, especially for the team's traditionally working-class core of fans. Doug Bukowski, a Chicago writer and member of Save Our Sox, points out that Comiskey's architecture was designed to blend with neighboring Bridgeport's working-class feel. Its arches, which extended around the old ballpark, "suggest the windows of a church or one of the multistory factories that were once so common here," Bukowski writes in *Baseball Palace of the World*, his sometimes humorous, ultimately wrenching look at the old stadium's last season. "[Charles] Comiskey put his ballpark in the middle of a neighborhood filled with people no more than a generation removed from the fields of the old country. They still viewed life the way peasants did and sought connections between work and play and worship. Comiskey provided that with his ballpark."[2]

Members of SOS canvassed outside the old stadium, trying to attract sympathetic White Sox fans to their petition campaign and their membership ranks. And many were drawn in that way. Newton Suewe was in graduate school at the time and attended many games at Comiskey. "One day I went to a Sox game," he remembers, "and there were some radicals out there protesting, trying to form an organization called Save Our Sox, and before I knew it I was one of the radicals."

Although he had always been interested in politics and sympathetic to liberal and progressive causes, Suewe had never been involved with a grassroots group like SOS before. As was true for many of the group's members, he found this an issue that cut close to home. "You almost feel like, 'Geez, is sports that important to me?' And in a sense yes and no. It sort of struck to close to home."

In his book, Bukowski writes of his first SOS meeting, in November 1986. Attendees were asked what had brought them to the organization. "One man stood up in a room full of strangers and said that whenever he got really depressed, he liked to drive by the ballpark; it made him feel good. No sky-boxes or playoff tickets or official team products necessary, just a swing by the park."[3]

"I also looked at it as a political and social issue," Bukowski says now, "like, we're going to be using tax dollars to build a new stadium. Corporate welfare. If some other company...if I knew they were getting corporate welfare, would I get involved in an organization? Probably not. I'd be upset about it, but I probably wouldn't get involved.

"Baseball and sports no longer mean what they once did," continues Bukowski, with more than a hint of bitterness. "They've transformed themselves into a major entertainment industry, grossly amoral, which I find offensive. What I was doing, in retrospect, was objecting to that, trying to perpetuate sports as I had thought they existed during my childhood and youth."

"I always felt like I was a part of it because it was my soul speaking out," Aranza says. "It was taking away my youth, and I'm sure it was for other people. Taking away their touchstone, taking away their tradition. Like losing somebody—you know that some things maybe are inevitable, but it's wrong the way it happened. Or you grieve, and you know you'll always grieve, and I do."

In their flyers, petitions, and public statements, SOS argued that the team could obtain any needed amenities by simply renovating the historic old park. "Should all of Chicago…be in the style of the Loop and suburban expressway corridor buildings, with windows that don't open, 24-hour security guards, and steel-and-glass vertical ice cube trays?" read a glossy SOS pamphlet distributed in 1987. "Or is there a place for Comiskey Park, with its tubular railings and wooden seats and overhangs like the balconies of the long-lost neighborhoods of our youth?"[4]

To that end, they campaigned and petitioned, held public meetings and lobbied their legislators. At its peak, the group was able to generate 5,000 signatures on its petition to preserve the stadium, and some positive press coverage.[5] But its core membership was never very large.

Bukowski thinks there are several reasons why there never was a massive outpouring of citywide support for the group and its cause. "The fan base for the White Sox tended to be blue-collar. And blue-collar America since the 1970s has taken it on the chin. People with mortgage concerns, job concerns, aren't going to have the psychic capital to expend on stadium issues, no matter how much they love the ballpark. They've got bread and butter to worry about." It also probably helped that the Chicago newspapers waged an all-out campaign to support a new stadium. In 1986, the *Tribune* editorialized: "The ailing mid-South Side needs the economic boost it will get if the rundown Comiskey Park is replaced with an attractive, multi-use stadium."[6] Without economic figures to back up its contention, the *Tribune* turned to more ephemeral claims: "The value of a professional sports team to an urban area is difficult to measure in dollars and cents. The jobs and tax revenue generated may not look impressive in hard figures. But add in what the presence of the team contributes to the overall attraction of living in the area and visiting it, and it becomes immense."[7] That the neighborhood already had a renowned facility, one that with some renovation costing far fewer dollars could provide just that appeal, was ignored.

But, of course, some working-class Chicagoans did get involved with the campaign—united, more than anything, by a feeling that in losing the historic ballpark they were losing part of their collective memory.

Comiskey Park was built on what was once, in the 1880s, a public dump. Legend has it that infielder Luke Appling once tripped over something during a game in the 1930s. Play was stopped, and when the grounds crew went to investigate by raking the infield, they found he had stumbled over an old teapot coming up out of the dirt. Some 50 years later, John Aranza snuck into the demolition site of his beloved stadium. "I went down in these deep trenches, which were way over my head, and on the sides of these trenches are layers of history, layers of earth. Bricks, wood, bottles. And I was just picking up things to verify what Comiskey was, even before it was built." There's still a note of wonder in his voice, almost ten years later. "I found an old saucepan, in a more shallow trench where they took out the left field wall."

Though it was rusty, Aranza could see that the saucepan was a blue and white speckled pot—a leftover design from a bygone era. Familiar with the Appling tale, and so many other Comiskey Park legends, Aranza was overwhelmed by the history he had just uncovered. "And I thought to myself, my God, like Aladdin's lamp I'm holding in my hands, just verifying a wonderful piece of baseball lore."

In the Bulldozer's Way

And then there were the residents of South Armour Square, low-income and elderly, whose very homes were threatened because of Reinsdorf and Einhorn's plans. The owners of the White Sox had initially hoped to pull their team out of South Armour Square, the inner-city neighborhood that along with Bridgeport surrounded Comiskey Park, using the need for a new stadium as a chance to get into what was assumed would be a more profitable suburban location.[8] First targeting the southwest suburb of Addison, Reinsdorf and company promised significant benefits if residents voted for the proposed stadium in a local advisory referendum: The state would supposedly receive $100 million in annual economic activity, and 2,500 jobs would be created.[9] But White Sox management ran into strident opposition in Addison. Local residents, worrying about a destructive change in their quiet community, and local environmentalists, fearing a threat to the region's nationally protected wetlands, were organized and vocal in their opposition. After an unfavorable referendum vote, the White Sox owners turned their sights elsewhere.[10]

As location after profitable location proved unworkable, the team had little choice but to return to the same neighborhood it had months earlier rejected as economically unsound and physically unsafe. But rather than choose to renovate the existing ballpark, Reinsdorf and Einhorn went forward with plans for a new Comiskey Park—across the street from the existing stadium. The only problem was, there was already something across the street—dozens of private homes and a good handful of businesses belonging to the overwhelmingly black, overwhelmingly low-income residents of South Armour Square.[11]

Hallie Amey and many other residents first learned of the proposed construction in a newspaper article. Although as part of public housing her apartment wouldn't be subjected to the city's eminent domain claims against much of the neighborhood, she worried for her private homeowner neighbors, and for the future of her already isolated community. (With the Dan Ryan Expressway to its east, Comiskey Park on its north, and railyards at its west side, South Armour Square was particularly cut off from the rest of the South Side.)[12]

Amey was at an advantage when it came to political experience. She and other residents of the Wentworth Gardens housing project were part of Wentworth Residents United for Survival, a neighborhood group that had taken on the government once before. In 1986, concerned about deteriorating conditions in their buildings' physical plant, residents worked with Sheila Radford-Hill, a longtime grassroots activist, to successfully battle the Chicago Housing Authority for more funds to repair their apartment buildings. From that struggle emerged the fledgling residents' coalition, with a victory under its belt providing it with the "vision and strength to organize," according to Radford-Hill. Now, with the threatened demolition of their neighbors' homes, the public housing activists were determined to organize the community once again.

They formed the South Armour Square Neighborhood Association, Amey explains, "to try to save ourselves, try and save our homes, and try and save the homeowners. Now we were concerned about ourselves, but we were really concerned about them, because these were individual homeowners and many of them were old and had spent years establishing a home where they would have someplace to live in their old age."

United by their desire to see Comiskey Park remain, the South Armour Square Neighborhood Association reached out to Save Our Sox. Some members from both groups attended one another's meetings to share in their common concerns and brainstorm together.

"We welcomed them and they welcomed us. Made our group a little bigger," Amey recalls with a laugh. "And we all had the same goal. We were not fighting against progress and all of that. We was just fighting for the right to keep homes for people…and many of those old folks lost their homes, and many of them did not live very long."

The Good Fight

"We were allied with the neighborhood people," John Aranza says. "Now, the community there was all black. And here's white people, black people united for a common cause. The people I was with I never met before. I didn't know them, they didn't know me, but it was something we all looked at ahead of us, our goal. And we didn't look at each other as our background, religious, job status, color, or anything. We had a goal."

Radford-Hill agreed to work with the residents of South Armour Square to try to save their community from the city's eminent domain claims—despite the fact that "most people in the city told me it was a done deal, and forget it." A dispute between the governor and the mayor of Chicago over who would be on the board of the newly created sports facility authority gave community activists some much needed time— a delay of almost a year. At a community meeting, Radford-Hill asked if "we want to work together over these nine months to try to stop this thing, and if not at least try to get a better deal...and they were willing to work, basically two years, around getting them a better deal. They got a better deal."

"Our chances were slim to none," Radford-Hill recalls. But the community had also seen how Addison area residents had successfully organized against having a stadium built in their neighborhood. And so the group went forward, Radford-Hill explains, "demonstrating on Reinsdorf's lawn, difficult to do with a bunch of senior citizens, but we did disrupt meetings, we had a press strategy. The idea was to make enough noise and be irritating enough that you could eventually blow the deal."

The group held protests at Comiskey Park and at City Hall. At a mock funeral set up by the group at a local school, attendants mourned the death of a community, reminiscing about the good times they'd shared as residents of South Armour Square. In the end, the neighborhood coalition wasn't able to stop the destruction of 178 privately owned housing units and 12 community businesses. But it was able to secure payments of market value plus a $25,000 cash bonus and moving expenses for the homeowners being displaced.[13] For those who were being forced to leave, there was some solace in having struggled for a better deal. For those with no choice but to watch their isolated community be further destroyed, it was a harder pill to swallow.

"There was a split at the end of the struggle, which, I think, robbed the residents of a sense of triumph," says Radford-Hill. "When the settlement deal was arrived at between the sports authority and the residents, the sports authority took the position that they were not interested in the community. They were only interested in the homeowners, the people that were actually losing their property. So they effectuated a split, and I think that kind of robbed the residents of a sense of victory."

Those residents who stayed filed a class action suit against the sports authority, state, and city. Forty-nine plaintiffs signed on to the lawsuit, alleging that the new stadium site was selected in violation of their civil rights. If the new stadium had been built north of where it ultimately was, they argued, there would have been fewer businesses and homes displaced. That wasn't done, according to the lawsuit, because the homes that would have been destroyed belonged to white residents.[14]

"Basically the suit lost," explains Radford-Hill. While not denying that individual residents may have suffered, the court entered a summary judgment on behalf of the defendants in the case. The judge also warned he would stick the Armour Square residents with the court costs if they appealed the decision. "So that effectively ended it," according to Radford-Hill.

Amey and her fellow activists were able to ensure that the nearby school, threatened by flying dust from construction of the new stadium, would have air conditioning installed. And residents of the nearby T.E. Brown apartments had their utility bills paid for by the sports authority for the first year of construction. But "the residents of Wentworth Gardens basically got nothing," says Radford-Hill—they received no monetary compensation, and they were forced to watch their neighboring homes and business destroyed. Still, Radford-Hill points out, Wentworth Residents United for Survival remained an organized, and even more experienced, group. "They became a resident management organization. Now they're in line to manage their own development."

Amey acknowledges the defeat, but not any surrender. "But if you have to survive, you don't have time to get discouraged. You don't. You don't have time....Oh gosh," she pauses with a chuckle. "Nothing, nothing, nothing could discourage me. I will just work and fight."

The Plot Thickens

For as long as the terms of the debate remained on White Sox demands for a new stadium, SOS had a focused fight. But Reinsdorf wasn't about to let the city off easy, so he and other White Sox officials went from hinting at the team's fleeing for greener pastures to actually taking well-publicized trips to Florida to check out the Tampa/St. Petersburg area. (St. Petersburg had, with public money, built a 43,000-seat baseball stadium in 1988—without having a professional baseball team. Anxious city officials actually flew White Sox executives in, on a Lear jet, to make the city's pitch—including a $10 million loan to Reinsdorf if the White Sox relocated—as the best new home for the Chicago team.[15]) But Reinsdorf, it would turn out, was only courting St. Petersburg at the suggestion of Illinois Governor Jim Thompson, who Reinsdorf would later reveal had encouraged him to threaten leaving Chicago if he wanted a new ballpark, saying, "It'll never happen unless people think you are going to leave."[16]

But no amount of renovations were going to be enough for Reinsdorf and Einhorn. They wanted a showpiece of a new stadium, and they wanted the taxpayers of Chicago to build it for them. Reinsdorf had always been fond of Royals Stadium in Kansas City, the 14-year-old home of the Kansas City Royals. Designed by the rising architecture firm of HOK, Royals Stadium was considered the first modern ballpark to break the unfortunate streak of perfectly circular stadiums so favored in the 1960s.[17] With its smaller seating capacity and waterfalls overlooking center field, the park was something of a refreshing architectural change, but its artificial turf and symmetrical dimensions soon became anathema to baseball purists.

Too Little, Too Late

By this time, stadium opponents had garnered enough attention to warrant a meeting with then-Mayor Harold Washington. When residents of South Armour Square went to meet with Washington in January 1987, Mary O'Connell and Doug Bukowski went along to present SOS's plans for renovations to the existing Comiskey Park. "He wasn't going to come out for the renovation of Comiskey Park if the White Sox were insisting they'd leave," Bukowski recalls. "Because then he would be branded as the mayor who didn't care and lost the White Sox. So he just let the whole process continue, which it then did under two other administrations."

It was at that time, when the threat of the team leaving the city seemed very real, that SOS shifted its focus—and lost its original core members. Newer recruits suggested that the group take a lobbying trip to Springfield, the state capital, to lobby for construction of a new South Side home for the team—at the cost of losing the old Comiskey, and the neighborhood homes of South Armour Square. The organization even received a check from one of the minority owners of the team, with the intent that it be used to lobby to keep the White Sox in Chicago.

"Because of the whole anxiety that the White Sox would produce with their threats to move, there was this great crisis in the organization as to whether they should get on board and go to Springfield and lobby for the new stadium or not," Bukowski recalls. "I just said, this is wrong. I can't do it. So I left. Maybe this was the only time in my life I could see the future, and it didn't work. I said, this is wrong, corporate welfare....There was no reason to subsidize baseball. In fact it's going to be an inferior replacement....People are not going to be able to see baseball the way they had seen baseball for 80 years. And this has proven true."

"You never win by appeasement," says Aranza, who also left the group at that time. "You never win." What had started as a struggle to save a cherished community landmark ended in bitterness for many involved in their first grassroots struggle. "Go over there and see what the hourly wage actually is, what they're charging for hot dogs," Aranza says in disgust. "It's obscene. They're making obscene profits."

The intensive lobbying of team officials and major league baseball higher-ups, combined with high-pressure tactics to prove their threat to yank the team was legitimate, proved too much for the Illinois State Legislature. In a midnight session on June 30, 1988, the body approved construction of a new stadium, with $150 million coming from state bonds and the rest from a two percent hotel tax.[18] (In fact, it was an after-midnight session, as Governor Jim Thompson had the clock turned off at 11:59 to avoid hitting a midnight deadline.[19]) The White Sox would only have to pay rent at their new home if attendance surpassed 1.2 million a year. "It was just an outrageously lavish lease agreement, and that has become industry standard," says Chicago architect Philip Bess, who drew up blueprints for a compromise new stadium that would have been less destructive to the neighborhood and cheaper to build.

To add insult to injury, once a new home was approved, team owners were determined to milk nostalgia for the old Comiskey Park for as long as it still stood. Thus, a ticket brochure before the 1989 season read: "With the dawn of this new era, we pause to reflect upon the past glory days of historic Comiskey Park. Nineteen eighty-nine and 1990 are dedicated to remembering the past combined with anticipation of a bright, exciting future in the new state-of-the-art stadium." Or, as one ad read in the local papers: "'The last season in historic Comiskey Park. Years from now, you'll say you were there.'"[20]

Out of the Ashes

By 1991, Reinsdorf, now the principal owner of the team, had his new home—the new Comiskey Park. The old Comiskey is a parking lot, and those surviving South Armour Square homeowners have moved elsewhere. What was once a close-knit working-class African-American community—with successful businesses and longstanding neighborhood ties—has been destroyed. Only the residents of the two housing projects remain. And what was once one of the country's most charismatic sports facilities is no more. In the new stadium, many of the old Comiskey's charms have been virtually eliminated.

"The last row in the upper deck of the old Comiskey Park, the very last row, behind the plate, was closer to the field than the first row of the upper deck in the new Comiskey Park," Doug Bukowski points out. Even the one idiosyncratic holdover from the park's Bill Veeck days, the stadium's "exploding" scoreboard, has a new twist—it abuts the back of the T.E. Brown apartments, whose senior residents must deal, even late at night, with its cacophony of sounds. Architecturally, says Bess, the new Comiskey "was the trial run" for the fledgling HOK architecture firm, which went on to design most of the new stadiums of the 1990s. "And Jerry Reinsdorf bought the trial run." Whether he now regrets it is another matter—the new Comiskey has been roundly criticized by baseball purists and fans, and attendance has slipped.

To this day, many of the original members of Save Our Sox refuse to go to games at the new Comiskey Park, or will only go if someone gives them a ticket. "I've never paid in the six years it's been open," says Bukowski. "I refuse to."

"If I have a fantasy about all this," Bess confesses, "it's that Comiskey will be economically obsolete, which in a way it already is, and that they'll build another one and do it right."

With the demolition in full swing, Aranza couldn't stay away from the site of so many memories. "As they were tearing down the ballpark, I would sneak in there at night," he explains. "Once I took [friend and fellow SOS member] Hank Trenkle. Him and I went in one night when the park was half down, and we sat in the bleachers. He brought his tape of the '59 World Series. And we're up there with half the park demolished, looking out at 35th Street with all the cars, looking down, and with the sunflowers growing in the middle of the field, some bunches of the sunflowers were bigger than us. And the jangled tubing of the railing, the wreckage out there, and we're just thinking of what was. And I know you can't live on those feelings, but it was just kind of, it was bitter and soothing at the same time."

Every year, at least once, the old core of Save Our Sox gets together to catch up and reminisce at Hickory Pit, an old restaurant near the stadium that had been the site of several SOS meetings. Many in the group have remained friends and have retained a sense that it was a good fight.

Looking back, John Aranza has no regrets about taking that pillowcase sign to Comiskey Park and the struggle that followed. "So help me God, I knew I did the right thing," he says. "And I overcame something and I achieved something in myself, for a cause and for a purpose and for the team. If anybody has a feeling that something is wrong and they want to change it or correct it or right it, in a decent and proper way, by all means do it. Because you'll go to your death saying, 'I wish I could have done more. I should have done something.' But I learned it that day."

8 BAD NEIGHBORS

> "To speak logically about the effects of sports facilities on community development should be to speak as much about community as about development."
> —CHICAGO ARCHITECT PHILIP BESS[1]

> "The pride and the presence of a professional football team is far more important than 30 libraries."
> —BALTIMORE RAVENS OWNER ART MODELL[2]

There were alternatives to new Comiskey. Hellmuth Obata Kassebaum, the architects contracted by the White Sox to build their new ballpark, may dominate new stadium construction, but they can't stop other would-be sports architects from proposing alternatives to HOK's assembly-line blueprints. Detroit had its John and Judy Davids with their Cochrane Plan, which would have saved both public money and a national landmark. Chicago had Philip Bess.

Bess looked at the planned demolition of Comiskey Park and saw as much a challenge as a potential tragedy. If the White Sox owners were insistent in their demand for a new stadium, he reasoned, why not take the opportunity to see something positive and productive come out of their blackmailing of the city? An architect and teacher in Chicago, Bess set out to design a ballpark that would reverse the trend started in the 1960s of isolating sports facilities from their surrounding neighborhoods and would instead be truly urban—a facility that would provide an anchor for a neighborhood revitalization that served not just visiting sports fans, but local residents as well.

Especially since Baltimore's Camden Yards was built with an eye to the ballparks of yesteryear, new "old-fashioned" ballparks have been in favor. These modern structures are meant to mimic the historic stadiums of baseball's glory days—minus the old-fashioned ticket prices, of course, and equipped with luxury boxes and club seating. Sports commentators and journalists are quick to wax poetic about the new old-fashioned facilities, playing up their contemporary role in the romantic lure of baseball.

And truthfully, for many sports fans—baseball fans in particular—it is difficult to argue with the criticisms of the crop of "modern" circular stadiums that popped up across the country in the 1960s and '70s. Those cement bowls weren't very interesting aesthetically, and they weren't particularly fan-friendly. Three Rivers Stadium in Pittsburgh, Cincinnati's Riverfront Stadium, and Veterans Stadium in Philadelphia, along with their domed counterparts in Houston, Minnesota, and Seattle, were built to hold as many people for as many sports as possible, with cheaply maintained Astroturf replacing fresh grass, and bland circular seating charts that placed fans equally distant from football or baseball games.

Unlike football, basketball, or hockey, for which there are precise standards that vary not at all from facility to facility, so much of the baseball viewing experience is about the sights, smells, and sounds of the stadiums in which it is played. In their sterile uniformity, the new generation of baseball stadiums lost the intricately designed angles and crevices of the playing field and spectator seats that used to make no two stadiums alike (and wreak havoc on pitching records and batting averages).

Accepting the destruction of the magnificent Comiskey Park as a foregone conclusion, Bess began work on an alternative to the plan being presented by White Sox owners and the city. His proposed stadium, Armour Field, was designed—in size, cost, and community function—to more faithfully reflect the traditional ballparks of yesterday. Instead of mimicking Royals Stadium, the suburban stadium in Kansas City that White Sox owner Jerry Reinsdorf so desperately wanted a replica of, Armour Field was designed to anchor a revived network of public places and community businesses. Instead of throwing out years of evocative and responsive architecture, Armour Field would be a chance to, at a more modest cost, re-create what was so special about the feel and function of old urban baseball stadiums. "For thirty years," Bess wrote in a description of his plan, "the solution to urban ballpark ills has been urban renewal and the suburban stadium—a dubious practice, analogous to prescribing chemotherapy for a broken leg."[3]

Back to Basics?

"If you've lived in Europe," says Chicagoan Mary O'Connell, "you know that people try to save the best of the old. There's not this endless thing of rip it down and build another, rip it down and build another. Some of the most beautiful and attractive parts of European cities are the older sections, where people have saved them and invested in them over time. And Americans go to Europe to see the buildings, to go drink in the pub that's been there since the 16th century, or worship in the places where people have been worshipping for hundreds of years."

In the United States, O'Connell and her fellow members of Save Our Sox soon found, historic landmarks are often torn down for the sake of progress. In the world of stadium architecture, and especially baseball stadiums, the irony goes a bit deeper. In the last ten years, both old and relatively new base-ball or multi-use sports stadiums have been razed—in order to make room for more "old-fashioned" replacements. The archi-tectural facades of urban baseball stadiums cherished for their convenient community locations, fan-friendly seating, and low-cost entertainment experience are being copied—even as the infrastructure of old neighborhoods that used to support them is being eroded or forever altered.

The baseball stadiums built in the first half of the 20th cen-tury were built right in bustling urban neighborhoods—lively communities like Brooklyn's Flatbush, Chicago's South Side and Boston's Kenmore Square. They were places families could walk to on summer afternoons, places businessmen could get to by taking public transportation, places kids could sneak into on a Sunday afternoon.

"The older ones were not only located in a network of streets and blocks, but they were constrained by the existing network of streets and blocks," Bess points out. "When you go to Fenway Park or Wrigley Field, the parks are literally kind of shoehorned into the block, in such a way to maximize seating capacity within a finite site. And one of the consequences of that is that you get these sort of odd, idiosyncratic kinds of playing field configurations, like the Green Monster in Fenway, and like the wells in left field, the higher center field bleachers, that you find in Wrigley. And those are a direct con-sequence of the site constraints."

Those idiosyncratic constraints, combined with individuali-ty in design, gave each old ballpark a unique character and feel. Ebbets Field was located in a bustling Brooklyn communi-ty of homes and businesses, with a DeSoto car dealership and a gas station behind its famous right field wall. Built into an already established neighborhood, it had a center-field wall that was a mere 384 feet from home plate—and that served as a constant advertisement for Schaefer beer (the H in the word

SCHAEFER lit up for hits, the E for errors).[4] The Polo Grounds in Manhattan, with center-field bleachers once called "the cigar boxes" for the Irish immigrant fans who crowded in them, had an outfield wall a staggering 505 feet from home.[5]

Like grand old theater houses or performance halls, these historic stadiums each had a unique character and feel that were as much a part of the baseball experience as the game itself. Seeing Luciano Pavarotti at Carnegie Hall, after all, is not the same as seeing him at Tanglewood. There's a different experience to Bob Dylan at Woodstock than at the Village Vanguard. And certainly Shakespeare performed at the Globe Theater in England has a different feel to it, different sensory and auditory and emotional components, than the same lines performed by the same actors at the local YMCA.

Team owners, meanwhile, latch on to the trend of "old-time" urban ballparks predominantly for the sake of increased profits. Luxury boxes, concessions revenues, and naming rights are their holy grails, after all, and when these revenue producers come into conflict with the requirements of an "old-time" ballpark, modern conveniences win the day.

Can't Tell the Players Without a Telescope

One reason, to be sure, has to do with upgraded standards of comfort as well as the relentless search for new sources of revenue. In the old steel ballparks such as Ebbets Field, the seating capacity was low, often 30,000 or fewer; and the seats were narrower, with less leg room. Modern ballparks required many more seats and more spacious accommodations—especially for the high-paying patrons who would be the new stadiums' most lucrative asset. "You put in club seats, those have even more leg room and wider seats than normal for today," architect and stadium historian John Pastier explains. "And they usually have to be in a discrete location, which means a deck of their own, and that starts pushing the upper deck away. Then you have all these suites that nobody ever thought of before, and they take up a bunch of space."

The result: In the typical new ballpark, additional layers—in the case of Jacobs Field in Cleveland, as many as three—of luxury suites and club seats are inserted, raising the upper deck skyward. Because support columns, which allow decks to be stacked more closely at the expense of a few obstructed-view seats, are anathema to modern stadium designers, the upper deck must be cantilevered further back from the field—and because a higher deck must be more steeply angled at the same distance from the field, they are moved back still further.

As a result, as frustrated fans have observed and researchers like Pastier have verified, most fans in the new ballparks are much farther from the action than they were in traditional ballparks. The back row of the upper deck in old Comiskey Park, with columns and no luxury levels, was closer to the field than the first row of new Comiskey's upper deck, which sits atop a wall of glassed-in suites. Old Comiskey was 75 feet high; new Comiskey soars 146 feet above the streets of the South Side.

The same is true in modern stadiums across North America. In upper deck seats in SkyDome in Toronto, fans can't even see large portions of the playing field.[6] Even the sterile '60s stadiums score better on Pastier's scale than popularly praised new "old-time" ballparks like Jacobs Field and The Ballpark at Arlington in Texas; in exchange for steel and brick and quirky angles, fans had unwittingly subjected themselves to some of the worst seats in sports history.[7]

Moving the upper decks up and away from the field has another important side benefit to team owners: It dramatically increases the stadium's volume. "Behind and under the seats, all that space has been growing astronomically," notes Pastier.

"There's more space for people to move around; there's much more space for selling them things."

"If I say 'Municipal Stadium,'" says Bess, invoking the name of Cleveland's recently demolished ballpark, "what would be some of the adjectives that come to mind? Cavernous. Well, cavernous Municipal Stadium, which seated 78,000, is almost equal in its footprint [the acreage taken up by an architectural project] to Jacobs Field, which seats 42,000. The seats in the upper deck at Municipal, even with that upper deck of seats that goes way back, are closer than they are at Jacobs."

All that extra space has significantly added to the bloated costs of current stadiums—and not just because of the extra land and construction costs inherent in a larger stadium. "In the new Comiskey Park," Bess explains, "the kinds of things they wanted in the building that are ancillary to the stadium—the dugouts and the lockers and stuff like that—did not fill up all that horizontal space that was created because of the design. In other words, there was a lot of extra space that was created in the new Comiskey Park that was not programmed, and not finished."

When that same design was mimicked in later stadium projects by HOK, the leftover space was filled with such costly extras as enormous and expensive workout rooms for players. Once the land was procured, says Bess, there was little excuse not to fill the space, even though it added still further to construction costs. "All of this is a consequence of literally a lack of physical constraint on where you build ballparks," Bess says, "and on how you build them."

This tremendous increase in sheer bulk—the typical new stadium of today has double the footprint of an older ballpark—is one reason why construction costs have soared in recent years, from as low as $25 million in the late 1960s to $300 million and up today.[8] Even if you were to completely re-create the few remaining old-time stadiums, and even adding luxury boxes as an economically necessary modern amenity,

Bess and others believe cities could save a huge amount of money just by following those same historic space constraints. "If you were to build Wrigley from scratch," says Bess, "it would cost between 70 and 80 million dollars."

"Unless you have a client that is passionately committed to building a good ballpark, you're not gonna get a good ballpark," says Pastier. In his estimate, of the five new baseball stadiums opened since 1991, Camden Yards is the clear winner. The Orioles, he explains, were willing to make some tradeoffs. "They combined the suites and the club seats. That helped reduce the height of the thing." At Pastier's suggestion, they cut down on the number of rows in the upper deck—"one way to get the worst seat in the house closer to the field is by removing it"—and made up the seating by extending the grandstand further into left field. "Which I think was an improvement, anyway. The old parks tended to have one full upper deck in the outfield if not two. That helps enclose the space and just creates a much better feeling." Camden Yards also features slightly tighter legroom than some other ballparks, further shrinking the depth of the grandstand.

Still, the discrepancy is not that great, and the view from the last row of Camden Yards is more like watching a game from a helicopter than sitting in an older park like Tiger Stadium, or even Memorial Stadium, which the Orioles abandoned for Camden Yards. "You put kids up there where they can't see," argues Chicago writer Doug Bukowski, "they get bored. And you don't make them baseball fans. Which means when they become adults, they don't want to go. Which means in the long run baseball, by pursuing these types of new stadiums, is only eroding its fan base."

Courting Food

Another area where the character and community feel of old-time stadiums is being eroded by today's sanitized monoliths is in food services. Any self-respecting 1990s stadium features a huge food court—oftentimes a "foods of the world" hodge-podge where fans are encouraged to buy German sausages, Tex-Mex tacos, and a wide array of international beers. Modern food facilities can ring up millions of dollars a year in added revenues for a team. Boston's Fenway Park has had its own equivalent for years with its tiny outdoor vendors who crowd together outside the stadium's venerable gates, selling every-thing from hot meats and drinks to touristy T-shirts. And yet Fenway's homespun marketplace is now under fire by team officials, who have lamented the state of the antique park for several years as the first part of a drive to tear it down.

Fenway Park, with its renowned Green Monster outfield wall and brick-and-steel single-deck grandstand, has drawn comparisons to cathedrals along with nightly sellout crowds. But, hemmed in by streets on all sides, it has few luxury boxes, little room for increased seating—and no space for expansive concessions areas or lush kitchen facilities.

Entrepreneurship, abhorring a vacuum, has provided where the Red Sox cannot. "Have you been to Fenway?" asks Pastier. "You've seen that thing along Landsdowne [Street, adjacent to the outfield wall] where Mama Mia has her homemade ziti and clam sauce on a little propane heater, right? And somebody else is making funnel cakes right before your eyes, and some-body else has jerk chicken from the Caribbean. I mean, that's the most wonderful thing that you'll find outside of any ball-park, and it makes the Red Sox crazy. That's one reason they want to be out of Fenway Park, because they see dollar signs evaporating before their eyes."

"It gets really comical," Pastier says. "These guys are sup-posed to be capitalists, and for the free market, but that's the last thing they want! They want to have a monopoly. The free market exists right outside of Fenway Park, and goddamn it, this is one time they're right: The free market is wonderful. Because it's a true free market, it's individual entrepreneurs doing their thing, and therefore providing variety and choice, at not huge cost."

For all the sense of variety, for all the attempts to re-create the spice of life that modern stadiums do in their multi-ethnic foodcourts, they are often all run by one snacks provider, usually one of the few big companies that dominate food courts in the entertainment scene. And for the exclusive right to sell in the modern sports palaces, those companies hand over a big share of their profits to team owners. In stadium design, as in every other aspect of professional sports ownership, profit is, and has always been, the bottom line. If artificially re-creating a sense of neighborhood helps in the process, then so be it. Oriole Park at Camden Yards features an outdoor walkway lined with souvenir shops and fast-food outlets—but *within* the stadium gates, for paying fans only and earning revenue for the team with every purchase. Jacobs Field features a private restaurant and an enormous team apparel shop that doubles as a history museum for the team. In the walkway between Jacobs Field and Gund Arena in downtown Cleveland, a lovely mosaic memorial has been installed. It honors, of all things, the once-thriving urban market that was destroyed in order to make room for the new sports facilities.

When the Seattle Mariners owners had to pick a location for their new stadium, notes Pastier, they had several sites to choose from, at varying distances from a popular shopping district. The team chose the most isolated location. "They'll certainly get more of the food and the drink and the souvenir sales," he says. "Once you go to the ballpark, you're so far away from those established businesses, you're much more likely to buy those things at the park itself. It's a captive audience situation." This, according to Pastier, is the explanation for why the White Sox moated the new Comiskey with 100 acres of parking, and why the Milwaukee Brewers refused to build their new ballpark downtown: Convenient access, it turns out, is less important than a captive audience for four-dollar hot dogs and five-dollar beers.

When more suburban sprawling stadiums seemed the better route to go, owners were all for them. But sometime in the design period of the new Comiskey Park, and before plans for Camden Yards were finalized, the trend in architecture, urban planning, and mall construction toward paying superficial homage to the America of yesteryear took center stage.

Nowhere was this more true than for HOK and the other leading stadium architects. "Right now there's a kind of mutually beneficial relationship between baseball owners and the architecture firms out of Kansas City and Seattle that do most of these jobs," Bess says. "The team owners say it has to be this way because the architects say it has to be this way; the architects say it has to be this way because the team owners tell us it has to be this way. That's sort of another major unrecognized scandal of the business. The corporate architects, the stadium architects, market their services to the tenants of these facilities rather than to the clients—that is to say, the people who pay for them."

What owner and architects alike missed along the way, however, was that it wasn't just their old-fashioned use of bricks or steel that made historic ballparks so popular and successful—it was their successful integration with the urban neighborhoods in which they were built. Indeed, though the similarities between the current crop of faux old stadiums and their historic counterparts are often emphasized by team owners and their media cohorts, it is their *differences* that are worth paying attention to. For it is the ways in which a Coors Field is dramatically different from, for example, a Fenway Park that tell us so much about the ways in which the increasing appetite for profits from owners and others shapes decisions about the games we play, the architecture we love, the way we are entertained. And this, finally, has as much to do with the changing face and function of the American city as it does with our favorite summer game.

Bad Neighbor Policy

Although Bess's plan would have also required the displacement of some residents—far fewer than the scores who lost their homes on behalf of the new Comiskey—part of the stadium design included the construction of new residences in previously vacant lots for those individuals who lost their homes. Far from being surrounded by parking lots, as the new Comiskey now is, Bess's proposed stadium would have been directly adjacent to a relocated city park (which would have stood on the grounds of the old stadium and even incorporated its old infield). It may have been this attempt at using the ballpark as a centerpiece of its surrounding neighborhoods that ultimately spelled Armour Park's doom, because in racially stratified Chicago, not everyone wanted to bring people together. The proposed stadium and adjacent public park were seen by some as a positive way of linking overwhelmingly white Bridgeport and predominantly black South Armour Square. Because access to the park would have been from South Armour Square, what had been a mostly white recreational area would become an integrated public space, and the neighborhood of Bridgeport would lose a buffer between it and its black neighbors.[9]

"My argument has always been that you can generate the kinds of revenues that are needed in today's sports economy with facilities that are both less expensive to build and put fans closer to the action," says Bess. "And so in that sense with respect to stadium design I'm more of a reformer than I am a revolutionary, because I'm not questioning entirely the premises of the existence of professional baseball. But I do think that where it becomes scandalous is when public moneys are supporting the industry to the extent that they do. And that there could be a lot less public expense involved that could result in better stadiums that still make teams the money that they need. It just wouldn't be squeezing every last little drop out of the lemon."

For Bess, the North Side Chicago neighborhood where Wrigley Field is located is a prime example of how stadiums and urban communities can interact—and an example of an increasingly rare successful *city* neighborhood. "There's 81 baseball games a year there, and it certainly is a national draw, people all over the world come to go to Wrigley Field, to that neighborhood," Bess explains. "But the neighborhood functions quite well the other 280 days of the year when there's not a game there. Within a five-minute walk from the pitcher's mound at Wrigley Field, you've got businesses, restaurants, schools, churches, convents, public transportation."

Those details are not unimportant to Bess and others concerned about urban life. "There's a whole city and the life that goes on there. There's a daily life to the neighborhood that exists independently of the ballpark. The ballpark enhances, and vice versa, but the notion of the city is the notion of a place where people live and work and hang out all the time."

In successful instances like Wrigley Field, the baseball stadium is not the be-all and end-all of a neighborhood's existence. In the new old-time ballparks of the 1990s, no such communities necessarily exist. And being a part of such urban neighborhoods is not what the new stadiums are about. They are attractions to go to, for people to get in their cars in the suburbs and spend a day at, before returning home. "Stadium construction is part of the same phenomenon as interest in casinos, interest in amusement parks," says Bess. "What's happened is that the 1990s city is implicitly being understood as an entertainment zone. And stadiums are part of this entertainment zone." Thus, says Bess, "to some extent all of the major corporate stadium architects market their services as providing entertainment. The assumption is that the city ought to be an entertainment zone because that's all it can be these days, because nobody really wants to live in the city. Whereas what I'm interested in is making the city better, understood in a traditional kind of way, where people actually live there as well as are entertained there.

"I certainly don't mind suburbanites coming in to go to baseball games," Bess continues. "Some of my best friends live in the suburbs. And I even understand political officials who are fairly desperate to keep revenues in the city. I certainly appreciate that dilemma. But I'm concerned about the way in which professional baseball, and stadium architects, are perpetuating this trend, the consequence of which is to reduce the notion of urban life to entertainment."

For Whom the Ball Wrecks

The problem, of course, is more than just a philosophical treatise on the purpose of cities. Not everyone has fled for the suburbs, and for those left behind—historically minority, working-class, and poor people—sparkling new sports stadiums and arenas represent both a luxurious form of entertainment and an appalling misuse of increasingly rare public funds. And, adding egregious insult to injury, in city after city, the new sports facilities are often funded by regressive taxes—by flat levies on consumer items that never take into account the consumer's economic status. Those most needing scarce urban funds to be directed toward improved schools, infrastructure, job opportunities, and the like are also footing a disproportionately high percentage of the construction bill. Those taxed the heaviest are the same abandoned urban residents least likely to be able to afford to go to the new stadiums. As Pastier points out, the proportion of cheap seats has steadily dwindled in the newer stadiums, with larger and larger sections reserved for club seats and other high-priced seating.

Bess's notion of the neighborhood ballpark also runs against the grain of urban development policy, which is increasingly concerned not with holding together communities but with creating high-activity "entertainment zones" that draw suburbanites and tourists back within the city limits. Starting in the 1960s, many cities began devoting an increasing amount of dwindling public resources toward construction projects geared toward downtown development and the white-collar market. Instead of putting money into housing or schools, cities looking for economic turnaround cast their eyes on ways to draw pocketbooks downtown: first with hotels, corporate headquarters, and the like, then as the decades passed, on to malls, museums, casinos, and other kinds of entertainment centers. The trend stretched late into the 1990s, in which the search for financial turnaround via downtown entertainment-based projects has become the norm—in everything from hosting the Olympics in Atlanta, to building a costly new arts center in Newark, N.J. Perhaps most pertinent for boosters of new stadium projects was the advent of downtown open-air malls (and sometimes fancy indoor ones as well), designed to imitate the historic districts that in many cases they wiped out while bringing in tourists and suburbanites with the promise of familiar shopping experiences.

In packaging urban history as a way of increasing consumer consumption, the faux old-time stadiums have much in common with the waterfront construction projects designed by developer James Rouse in the 1980s. Beginning with the overwhelming success of Faneuil Hall in Boston, Rouse went on to build the immensely popular Harborplace in Baltimore and the reconstructed South Street Seaport in lower Manhattan. Each of these projects re-creates a historic look—from cobblestone paths to historically designed storefronts and antique-looking signs—in order to reinvent the mall as an authentic walk down memory lane. That practically the only thing distinguishing one city's "historic" attraction from another's is the food selection at the chain restaurants within—crab cakes in Baltimore, chowder in Boston—and the city name on the Hard Rock Cafe T-shirts has not diminished these attractions' popularity.

M. Christine Boyer, a professor of architecture and urbanism at Princeton, points to the faux villages of Disneyland as the first blow for the "historic-marketplace tableau" that has proven so popular in urban centers. No matter where the Disneyland guest travels in the park, she points out, all roads lead back to Main Street USA and its stretch of souvenir stores. Thus, Boyer writes, "Disneyland is quintessentially a landscape for consumption, not for leisure. In just this manner, South Street Seaport is above all a marketplace, the stage for a particular kind of experience—that of pure desire, where the buyer imagines a fantastical world, which the possession of a certain object seems to promise."

Sites such as Rouse's South Street Seaport are "laden with historical allusions to the traditional vision of the city," writes Boyer, even as they end up contributing to the destruction of the modern American city in its most familiar form. "New York is no longer a city concerned with such high-Modernist aspirations as providing a broad range of housing, efficient public transportation, or leisure and work spaces for the masses."[10]

These "historic" shopping malls have replaced schools, libraries, and parks as the focus of municipal spending in nearly every American city. Now planners and developers use huge quantities of time, public money, and public space—and receive huge amounts of positive publicity—for new historic storefronts and new historic stadiums. The city itself has increasingly become an entertainment/consumption zone—one that aggressively milks nostalgic images of what the city should be in order to create an unprecedented consumer-based culture. In order to produce the spaces—physical, social, and economic—for such nostalgic projects, actual historic buildings and zones are simply destroyed.

The creation of a forced consumer nostalgia for an artificial past may have reached new levels of absurdity in central Florida, where the Walt Disney Company has opened a new town: Celebration, Florida. Although it has no actual history besides its swampland origins, in the promotional push for the development Celebration was billed as a "traditional" American town with a not-quite-real grand old history. As Russ Rymer writes in his compelling look at Celebration in *Harper's* magazine, "What Celebration was promising was the restoration of the aesthetic and communal values of pre-World War II America. The town rising out of the palmetto swamp would be the Experimental Prototype Community of Yesterday."[11]

From the inherent consumerism of Rouse's harbor projects and HOK's new-old stadiums comes the next step in the marketing of history and the blending of community with theme park. The town of Celebration, with its combination of six-figure homes and $600-a-month apartments, white picket fences and spacious walkways, is designed to trigger a nostalgia for an idealized American city that never was. There was even early talk at Disney that the town should have an invented history to provide it with "roots." As Rymer writes: "What Celebration celebrates, oddly, is an American community that existed precisely in that time before corporations made it their business to build communities—an era before neighborhoods became subdivisions and business districts became malls and culture in all its sources and manifestations became supplanted by the cathode-ray tube and the theme park."[12]

Changing Neighborhoods

It is impossible to watch a broadcast of a game from Camden Yards, or Jacobs Field, or Coors Field in Denver and not hear constant references to those glittering new stadiums as examples of architectural magic. (TV journalists seldom interview fans about the vast distance from their seats to the playing field.) More important, the facilities are repeatedly referred to as major components in their respective downtowns' "renaissance." And certainly, if the number of increased downtown buildings or the pedestrian traffic on game days or at attractive new bars is an indication, those cities have gone through urban renaissances. The problem is, when discussing a downtown revitalization and renaissance, no one ever mentions (or touches base with) the vast majority of working-class and poor residents of those same cities. (A glaring omission, but a not uncommon one. Maybe that has historically always been true of renaissances. It seems unlikely, after all, that 14th century peasants in Florence spent much time admiring art.)

What has happened to these former industrial giants, at the same time that their glittering new stadiums have helped make them official renaissance towns?

Bill Marker wonders just this as he visits one of Camden Yards' less fashionable neighboring areas, an old district known as Pigtown. He is mulling over some other uses the state of Maryland could have spent its $400 million in lottery money on instead of new twin stadiums for the Orioles and Ravens.

"When I worked representing parents and sometimes children in abuse and neglect cases, if you were losing your kids because of your drug use, we could get you into some sort of program," Marker says. "But if you're just generally out on the street and you say, yes, I've got a drug problem and I'm ready to deal with it, you should live long enough until there's a spot for you. And there's nothing more important than that. Not only in terms of the drug treatment, but guess what? If you had enough drug spots available, there'd be a lot of $15,000-a-year jobs for ex-junkies."

The impact on U.S. cities—particularly those unfortunate enough to have been long-centered on manufacturing and heavy industry—of decades of corporate pullouts, tax abatements, and redirection of public dollars into enormous consumer centers has been devastating. Expensive new stadiums, waterside malls, and development projects—the cornerstones of many an urban renaissance—have received massive public contributions. They've meant considerable public sacrifice in the form of gobbling up costly land without paying property taxes, taking over what were once true public spaces, and refocusing urban priorities.

Community groups have challenged these spending priorities in city after city. In testifying against spending public money on a new ballpark for the Minnesota Twins, Minneapolis Federal Reserve vice-president Arthur Rolnick recalls, "I said let's have a referendum on it, because if you're going to give this money to sports teams, it means you're not giving it to the schools, and you're not giving it to fighting crime or cleaning up your parks and your roads. And I suspect when you rank these things, the public would rank these much lower, but I said have a referendum. Now of course they didn't want to do that, because they didn't want to hear what the public had to say. They were pretty sure the public was going to vote against something like the Twins or the Timberwolves—they didn't have much support." In fact, a poll by the *Minneapolis Star Tribune* in January 1997 found that if given a choice of how to divide their tax money, citizens would spend it quite differently than stadium boosters: 44 percent for education, 29 percent for crime prevention, 13 percent for transportation, eight percent for the arts; a stadium ranked dead last, at six percent.[13]

Crumbling schools, staggering African-American infant mortality, and lingering unemployment are the undiscussed reality behind Cleveland's stadium-enhanced renaissance. "The result is what has been termed the *dual city*," writes Cleveland State University professor Dennis Keating, "in which downtown areas can thrive, and the white-collar sector mostly employing white suburban commuters can grow, whereas poor neighborhoods and their working-class and poor residents, especially blacks and Hispanics, do not share in this growth and must cope with high rates of poverty, unemployment, and other social problems."[14] Jacobs Field and Gund Arena were built with public money and their tenants given significant tax abatements on the property they were built on.

In the state of Ohio, property tax goes to public education, so the progress for wealthy owners is linked to further education cuts. Using numbers from the Cuyahoga County Auditor, the Cleveland Teachers Union charges that city schools lost more than $3.5 million in 1995 alone on tax abatements granted to Jacobs Field and Gund Arena.[15]

When it comes to the $450 million Gateway complex, Cleveland teacher Michael Charney was more outraged by the choice of funding recipient than by the tax abatement loss of dollars that the Cleveland schools so desperately needed. "The political corporate forces went for an increase in taxes on beer and wine and cigarettes," Charney points out, "and decided that the most appropriate use of those taxes was for a stadium complex—rather than for either dealing with social service problems or dealing directly with the capital problem of the Cleveland public schools falling apart physically."

The business community in Cleveland, and its political cronies, had a chance to "fix up those broken buildings, or hire social workers to deal with the kids' problems, or open up the schools at night," according to Charney, "so they [could] become stabilized institutions in a totally destabilized community." Instead, those same civic committees backed the funding of Gateway.

The problem extends far beyond former rust-belt headliners. In 1997 in Austin, Texas, a state senator proposed legislation that would end abatements on property taxes that fund schools. A study conducted by the senate's Economic Development Committee found that Texas schools lost almost $480 million in local property tax revenue from 1985 to 1995 because of tax abatements.[16]

For Charney and other longtime activists who've watched the shift in urban planning and emphasis over the past 30 years, the symbolic impact of costly new stadiums is enormous.

"I think that's more of a metaphor for a society's priorities than it is the actual drain on the actual cash," Charney says.

The same can be said for other entertainment zone specialties in cities such as Cleveland. After all, it's hard to persuasively argue that the public school children of Cleveland somehow benefit—besides by having an increased appreciation of Little Richard—from the placement of the Rock and Roll Hall of Fame on the shores of Lake Erie. In fact, because the museum was built on valuable property with tax abatements, the opposite could be argued—and has been, for decades, by local activists.

Charney, who's been a public school teacher for over two decades and active with the teachers union for the last ten years, wishes that "there were as much effort [put] into making sure that every child in Cleveland had a home library by the time they were in first grade, where they had ten or fifteen or twenty books that they owned, rather than just fixing up the stadium." He'd take it a step further and declare that "admission to a Browns, Cavaliers, or Indians game would be the price of a ticket plus a children's book. At least [for] the people in the loges." It certainly might be one way, in the current construction-crazy climate, to force a re-examination of urban values. "Just as there is a somewhat moral obligation that people don't starve," Charney argues. "I think there may have to be created a moral obligation that children have the right to be literate by the time they're seven or eight. And that's not only the problem of the narrowly defined public school system, but society at large."

The underfunding of Cleveland's school system is a daunting problem—one directly related to a shift in the city's priorities. "The legacy of that lack of capital investment shows up in the massive illiteracy of the adult population," Charney says. "The same people pushing these stadia are the same people who live in the suburbs, moved their businesses to the suburbs, and now say, 'Fix it, the schools are lousy.'"

Likewise, in Detroit, Bill Dow and other members of the Tiger Stadium Fan Club faced an uphill battle in trying to force politicians to look at the opportunities lost by putting so much emphasis on building a new stadium. "We kept saying, if you ask any urban planning expert, if you had that kind of public money to spend toward urban renewal, one of the last things they would say would be a baseball stadium that's used 81 days out of the year," Dow says. "But they just fell for it."

"There's a real desperation in Detroit," Frank Rashid points out. "I understand it—we all had that feeling when the Renaissance Center came, that one big thing is going to make the difference. It's the politics of desperation, and it's self-defeating. Finally, what we have to do is what you've got to do to rebuild a city: block by block, making sure that the business climate is right, planning carefully, and making sure that you're investing in things that are going to improve the quality of life for your people, to make your city an attractive place to live and work. It's not pretty, and it takes time. The problem with these big projects is when you invest everything in them you can't *do* the other stuff, there's nothing left. The lost opportunity is what's so frustrating, and so awful."

Structural Adjustment

Public money spent on private construction projects instead of social services, severe cuts in social welfare even as corporate welfare continues unchecked, growing inequities between the haves and have-nots, deteriorating quality-of-life-indicators in so-called renaissance towns—if these were part of urban planning in the Third World, they'd have a name: "structural adjustment."

In some ways, the public funding of huge stadium projects, outdoor malls, and casino halls, coupled with enormous cuts in local spending on social services, can almost be viewed as the domestic version of the structural adjustment plans pushed on developing nations (and increasingly Western Europe as well) by the World Bank and the International Monetary Fund. The formula is simple: Devote ever-decreasing amounts of public wealth to support the services needed by the poor and helpless, and invest more and more in ways that will return increasing profits to the small numbers of rich and privileged. Oftentimes in the Third World that has meant an emphasis on the tourist and export economy over more indigenous industrial or agricultural solutions.[17] A similar emphasis on tourists over residents is happening in city after city across the U.S. The new Comiskey Park was built with an eye for the outside baseball fan coming to the South Side to check out an exciting new attraction—not for locals, whose homes and businesses were destroyed as a necessary part of the process.

Seeing once-proud downtowns reduced to clamoring for tourist dollars is oddly reminiscent of Third World countries continually redefining themselves and their priorities, or being redefined, by their relationship to the almighty U.S. dollar. For years, development investment in Latin America and elsewhere has been linked to large-scale cutbacks in social services. Indeed, that link has been the cornerstone of World Bank and International Monetary Fund policies in much of the Third World. In U.S. cities, meanwhile, money becomes available for large-scale private projects like sports arenas or privately owned prisons at the same time that it's reduced for education, low-income housing, or public health services. Increasingly, the two are intricately connected—they don't just happen to occur coincidentally.

Indeed, if adjustment policies are forcing activists in the developing world into new strategies, their urban U.S. equivalent has inspired local activists to do the same. The Cleveland teachers' union organized a successful petition drive to place a referendum on the ballot in August 1997 calling for limits on tax abatement. Confronted by the links between downtown development and their deteriorating schools, a local union was stepping far past a traditional workplace issue to combat the current powers that be. "Gateway does not represent something new that 'we have'—it's rather treating Cleveland the way the rich nations treat the Third World," said one Cleveland radio commentator in the aftermath of the successful drive for a new football stadium. "Only instead of being dominated by foreign powers, we're dominated by a small group of powerful local people who manage to convince us that we are the beneficiaries when they are robbing us."[18]

The way in which local stadium projects are reported—the discussion of those ever-popular urban renaissances—also mimics in many ways U.S. press reports on the complicated economics and politics of Third World countries. When *The New York Times* writes that a Latin American country is doing well economically, it usually means that its exports are up, that profits to a small group of corporate or industrial elites are up as well, and that thus by its own definition of success the country's adjustment has been a success. Economic success is simply not connected to the actual well being of a majority of the population. Instead, a substantial percentage of the population simply becomes irrelevant when the discussion focuses on economic success. And the same can be said for cities such as Detroit, Cleveland, and Baltimore.

Baltimore has built its reputation as a renaissance city on one glorious project: the Inner Harbor. Ringed by numerous malls featuring the trendiest in retail shops and boutiques, and served by numerous adjacent hotels that have gone up over the past decade, and "water taxis" to take you to historic Fort McHenry (site of the "rockets' red glare" that inspired Francis Scott Key to pen "The Star-Spangled Banner"), Harborplace was among the first Rouse-designed architectural "triumphs." Just to the west of the harbor you'll find Baltimore's Otterbein neighborhood, one of the first experiments in state-sponsored gentrification, when the city filled houses vacated for a '70s

highway project that never came to pass by selling homes to
"urban homesteaders" for $1 a pop. And just west of *that* is the
culmination of Baltimore's redevelopment: Camden Yards,
complete with its own self-contained mall in the ground floor
of the old B&O warehouse, now redeveloped as a symbol of
urban revival through tourism.

Keep going west a few blocks past Camden Yards, and you're
in Pigtown, where, as in many other Baltimore neighborhoods,
among the most notable landmarks are the numerous pawn
shops. From here you can just see Oriole Park at Camden Yards
and its new football neighbor. One of the best vantage points
is Copper's Lot, a huge plot of vacant land cleared for urban
renewal. It remains vacant years later because of toxic wastes
left by the factory that formerly occupied the site, which the
city shows no great desire to clean up.

As others have argued before, the United States is increasingly a country whose economic system does not require that
the vast majority of people be employed. In the modern
American city with its modern old-time stadium, people who
go from suburbs to the ballparks, tourists who stay in area
hotels and take in a game for an afternoon, and even some successful downtown residential fans can pass by the people whose
needs are simply not counted. Urban planners can draw up
entire downtown developments while ignoring big chunks of
the population as if the local needy didn't exist.

And even when communities organize to stop new stadium
deals, they still face tremendous odds. That's certainly been the
case in three high-profile towns in the 1990s, where spirited
opposition by local activists, a determinedly resistant public,
and outrageous demands by team owners weren't enough to
stop the stadium juggernaut from rolling on.

9 REPEAT OFFENDERS

"Sports is a way of life, like eating. People say, 'You should pay to feed the homeless.' But the world doesn't work that way."
— MINNESOTA TWINS OWNER CARL POHLAD[1]

Credit Seattle's team owners and local politicians with audacity, if nothing else. In five years, the city's two professional sports franchises went up for sale, threatened to leave town, and wrangled huge public deals for new stadiums from a concerned populace. Twice they were met by a spirited, never-say-die opposition that maintained its multi-pronged attack long after deals were signed and funds committed. When the dust clears and the bonds are issued, the lawsuits thrown out of court and the public referenda ignored, King County taxpayers will be left with one of the most enormous sports debts in recent history—close to $1 billion and counting for new homes for the baseball Mariners and football Seahawks.

The first fight began in the early 1990s, over the fate of the Mariners. Saddled with what he claimed were insurmountable debts and a dwindling fan base, team owner Jeff Smulyan put the club up for sale in the winter of 1991. Early fears that the team would leave Seattle for greener pastures—presumably one of the southern cities then making overtures to major league baseball—were assuaged when the Baseball Club of Seattle bought the Mariners for more than $100 million in early 1992. The club, a compendium of local businessmen headed up by Nintendo officers, would need official league support—and some controversy did arise over partial foreign ownership of the "American pastime." But their bid was successful, and almost a year after buying the team its owners began pushing for a new baseball-only stadium to replace the not yet 20-year-old Kingdome.[2]

A September 1995 referendum to institute a sales-tax increase to fund a new Mariners stadium was narrowly defeated, but team owners were undeterred. They declared that by October 30 the state would have to come up with a commitment to build a new stadium, or else they'd put the team up for sale. Just in the nick of time an emergency session of the state legislature approved a plan for a $320 million stadium to be paid for with new taxes on restaurants and car rentals. It was a move that outraged those who'd already questioned the priority of funding a new public facility—and who thought they'd had a victory with the September referendum's defeat. "If the Mariners need a new stadium—if any private business needs to build a new factory—then find the money on the private market," says attorney Shawn Newman, who, on behalf of his citizen group CLEAN, sued the state, and ultimately lost.

Citizens for More Important Things was another grassroots group formed to oppose the public funding of a new stadium. Initially only three people at its founding in 1995, the group at its peak had 800 donors and approximately 4,000 volunteers, according to Chris Van Dyk, one of the organization's founding members. An investment broker and adviser, Van Dyk had an apparently boundless supply of energy when it came to taking on the stadium barons. "Every time they put up a dike to stop the flow of opinion," he once told *The Seattle Times*, "we know exactly where to dig a hole."[3]

By June 1996, the architectural plans had revealed yet another old-time stadium—this one with a retractable roof to ward off rainy Seattle days. But in large part because of the cost of that high-tech roof, within months the Public Facilities District created to oversee the stadium project had declared that the new stadium was going to cost some $45 million more than initial projections. Additionally, the retractable roof would not be ready for the venue's planned April 1999 opening.

Reaction was swift and concerted. Despite their push to see a new stadium built for the '99 season, the Mariners hadn't yet signed a lease for the new facility. Local politicians, no doubt wary because of public outcry over highly publicized cost overruns in such cases as Cleveland, wanted assurances that forking over an additional $45 million was really worth it. By December 1996, four city council members wrote a letter to the PFD, urging a delay of the stadium opening until these issues could be better examined.

The reaction from the Mariners was harsh and unequivocal. Within two days, team owners announced that they were selling the team and pulling out of the stadium project. In a statement read live on local radio, team owners declared, "Recently, after more than three years of work toward fulfilling the dream of thousands of fans, the Baseball Club of Seattle has concluded that there is insufficient political leadership in King County to complete the ballpark project in 1999. [The] owners of the Mariners take great pride in having fulfilled all commitments and obligations to those who looked to us to preserve Major League Baseball for Seattle. To them, and to everyone, we cannot explain why those who represent the people have chosen to let baseball go."[4]

The team owners declared they weren't interested in any more talks with King County officials, but like any good hostage takers, the opposite proved true. There wasn't much point in holding a gun to taxpayers' heads if team management didn't think they could ultimately get their way. Sure enough, within two weeks of the Mariners declaration, Republican Senator Slade Gorton had stepped in to broker yet another deal with team owners—this one handing the petulant bosses more profits and fewer expenses. Based on media coverage of the ensuing events, local officials could just as likely have been dealing with armed guerrillas at the governor's mansion as much as supposedly respectable local business owners. "Gorton helped persuade the owners to reconsider," *The Seattle Times* reported in one Christmas Day story. "He has urged governments to accede to the Mariners' demands and has criticized the city for its dealings with the team."[5]

Under the terms of the new deal, the city of Seattle would pay for police traffic control, cleanup, and extra transit and compensate the local neighborhood for the stadium's impact— all of which was originally supposed to be covered by the Mariners.[6] What had once seemed outrageous was about to become reality. The Mariners had their conditions met; ground was broken at the new stadium site in March 1997.

Give Them an Inch...

Meanwhile, with the Seattle Seahawks ownership in California businessman Ken Behring's hands for nine years, rumors surfaced that the team's position in northern Washington state was less than secure. "In Washington state," explains attorney Shawn Newman, "the worst thing you can be is a California developer." A local owner was needed, supposedly, to keep the team in town. But, once such a prospective homegrown buyer was found, he followed the pattern of local owners across the country.

When Microsoft co-founder and local billionaire Paul Allen expressed interest in buying the Seahawks in early 1996, he made one thing perfectly clear: A new stadium to replace the 20-year-old Kingdome was a necessary condition of his purchase. His interest was greeted with joy by many in the northwest community, despite the warning bells that hundreds of millions in public money was about to be requested once again. The hero worship was appalling to Newman. "They paint the local guy as the savior on the white horse," the Olympia resident says in disgust, "where we're picking up the droppings."

At hearings to determine the viability of another massive publicly supported project, Allen and other new stadium proponents rallied busloads of supporters to the state capital to express their enthusiasm. Shawn Newman, whose law offices are just down the street, took a stroll to the hearing to check out the scene and get his own two cents in. "They've got all these people drooling on themselves, testifying what a great deal it is," Newman recalls. "They never even read the damn bill, they don't know what they're talking about."

This was an emotional issue, pure and simple, and new stadium proponents had brought in the heavy artillery. "And I don't mean to criticize these people," Newman explains, his frustration evident. "They talk about how their sons or daughters are so enamored, that the Seahawks mean so much to them, that my little boy [has] leukemia and [is on] life support and that it was because the Seahawks had done something that had got him out of death's grip, or some bullshit."

Of course, Allen's call wasn't just for a facility to make the sick children of Seattle happy. Instead, the team's massive PR campaign emphasized the many uses of the new facility. They brought in representatives from the U.S. Olympic Committee to argue that such a venue would be ideal for hosting future Olympic soccer matches, quoting the commissioner of Major League Soccer to the same end.

When it was Newman's turn to speak, he told those gathered that "the real question you have to ask yourself is one of priorities, and whether or not the voters are going to respect you in the morning after you get done with another stadium shuffle. Because you want priorities." A bigger concern is that "40,000 legal residents of Washington state are going to lose their food stamps this summer. About 8,000 are going to lose social security benefits. Legal residents. That's an emergency, not building a new stadium for a billionaire."

By February 1997, Washington Governor Gary Locke had called for a statewide vote on the creation of a ten percent tax on licensed sports apparel and memorabilia in order to fund the public's share of the proposed $402 million new stadium.[7] When that proved controversial (as well it might, with apparel giant Nike based in neighboring Oregon) politicians agreed that the funding would instead come from an extension on the state's hotel/motel tax and a tax on Seahawks tickets and parking.

Allen himself had pledged at least $100 million toward stadium construction, and he now took the unheard-of step of single-handedly financing the statewide referendum—which ran him $4.2 million. Allen's supporters said that he did so only because state politicians had insisted that if there was to be another statewide vote, taxpayers would not be made to pay for it. But the step was an alarming one for many. "I just don't recall ever seeing someone pick up a total tab for an election," North Carolina political science professor Thad Beyle told *The New York Times*. "It bumps up against questions about just how far you can let democracy go."[8]

Paying for the election was a bold step for the billionaire in another way as well. "Paul Allen never voted in an election," claims Van Dyk. "The first election there's any public record of him having voted in is the election he purchased."

That vote, and those dollars, would be key in what would be the most expensive initiative campaign in state history. In June

1997 voters narrowly approved the new stadium for the Seahawks. For kicking in some $3 million, Allen got his $300 million-plus public contribution, and years of luxury box revenue from this new stadium. It apparently was money well-spent. Seattle is getting its two new facilities, and its taxpayers are going to be paying for them for a long time to come.

Minneapolis: Win a Few...

In the early '90s, Minnesota would have seemed an unlikely target for teams seeking new facilities, if only because it had two of the newest buildings around. The Target Center, built in 1990 with minimal public money, was home to the new Timberwolves basketball team. Just blocks away in downtown Minneapolis sat the Hubert Humphrey Metrodome, a fabric-roofed 64,000-seat stadium that housed both the baseball Twins and football Vikings.

The Metrodome itself was built mostly at public expense— $55 million of it, financed largely by hotel, motel, food, alcohol, and beverage taxes. The pitched battle between community activists and local business interests that surrounded its construction presaged some of the public stadium fights of the late '80s and '90s. Particularly at issue, remembers neighborhood activist Carla Bruenig, was the issue of housing, since many buildings were torn down to make way for parking for the new stadium, and traffic, which suddenly flooded into the local streets on game days.

The Metrodome was never a thing of beauty. During day baseball games the translucent Teflon roof made every flyball an adventure, and the Twins never did seem able to find the right artificial turf to prevent balls from bouncing twenty feet over outfielders' heads. But it quickly felt like home to the Twins and Vikings, especially during the Twins' two world championship seasons of 1987 and 1991, when fan noise inside the dome out-decibeled a jet taking off. With a new stadium firmly in place, Minnesotans could at least consider sports subsidy battles a thing of the past—doubly so when NBA expansion team owners Marv Wolfenson and Harvey Ratner spent $81 million of their own money (along with $23 million in public funds) to build the Target Center in 1990 for their new Timberwolves basketball team. Minneapolis-St. Paul was sitting pretty: one of only six metropolitan areas with franchises in all four pro sports leagues, and the only one with state-of-the-art facilities for each to play in. Throw in a generally strong, diversified state economy, and Minnesota's largest urban center had reason to brag.

Until the North Stars packed up and left town.

Minneapolis' hockey team had been playing in the Met Center in nearby Bloomington, and that suburban arena was suffering in both attendance and revenue because of competition from the new Target Center. The team's owners considered relocating to share the newer building with the Timberwolves, but instead opted to find an arena where they would collect a greater share of the revenue streams. They found one in Dallas, becoming the Dallas Stars in 1993, and leaving the publicly owned Met Center empty.

Meanwhile, the Target Center was facing a sudden cash crisis. Wolfenson and Ratner had counted on paying off the $35 million in construction costs with revenue from ticket and suite sales; but the building ultimately came in at $104 million, leaving "Harv and Marv," as they were universally known, with $10 million in debt payments and property taxes due each year on the arena and no way to pay it off. After the failed attempt to get the North Stars to relocate to the Target Center, the pair took a hard look at the sea of red ink and turned to the city government for a bailout.

To get the city's attention, Harv and Marv announced in the spring of 1994 that they were moving the Timberwolves to New Orleans for the upcoming season. The NBA rejected the move, but only on the condition that Minneapolis agree to spend $74 million to purchase the arena, financed largely by sales and property taxes at the arena—money that previously went directly into general city revenues. Wolfenson and Ratner, as part of the deal, sold the team to a local millionaire for $88.5 million, turning a 172 percent five-year profit on their original $32.5 million investment.[9] And despite promises by proponents that the buyout would help lure a new hockey team to Minneapolis, when the NHL announced its intent to expand to the Twin Cities in 1997, it was to a proposed new arena across the river in St. Paul, which would replace the 25-year-old Civic Center Arena. The seven-year-old Target Center, Minnesota Sports Facilities Commissioner Henry Savelkoul explained, no longer had the "provisions," in the form of revenue from luxury suites, advertising, and concessions, to support pro hockey.[10]

The Target Center bailout left the Minnesota populace wary of "economic development" subsidies—all the more so as it came on the heels of another notorious corporate giveaway involving Northwest Airlines. In 1992, the state legislature had granted Northwest Airlines an astounding $761 million in loans, tax breaks, and cash in exchange for a promise to build two maintenance bases in the northern part of the state. But as the legislators soon discovered, Northwest was in no position to build anything. Its new owners had severely overextended their finances in their leveraged buyout of the company, and Northwest had already lost $1 billion in the two years since. The company—which was "very close to bankruptcy," according to the Minneapolis Federal Reserve's Art Rolnick—promptly canceled the planned bases but kept the no-strings-attached state loans to help pay off their debts. "The [bases were] bogus," says Rolnick. "It was just a ploy to say, I'm going to give you jobs up north, an economically depressed area, if you loan me this money." Only after years of public outcry did Northwest finally agree to a scaled-back version of the plan that would create just 954 jobs, less than a quarter the number originally promised.

For a state with a long liberal and union tradition—Minnesota's state Democratic Party is known as the Democratic-Farmer-Labor Party—the Northwest deal was an expensive lesson in the costs of corporate welfare. The state responded by passing the Minnesota Corporate Welfare Reform Law in 1995, requiring that businesses that receive state or local economic aid must show net job growth for the state within two years, or else refund the money.[11]

Deals like these may have soured the public on subsidizing local business leaders with nine-figure expenditures, but it only whetted the appetite of Twins owner Carl Pohlad for the riches available via corporate welfare. Pohlad, despite a team that broke attendance records at the new dome, had often complained of feeling like a second-class citizen there. Seating in the multipurpose stadium was arranged more for football than for baseball, and, perhaps more important, the Vikings controlled all the luxury suite revenue, leaving the Twins to survive on ticket sales and concessions revenue alone.

In September 1996, Pohlad went public with his request for a new ballpark, hinting that he would activate an escape clause in his Metrodome lease if a new stadium was not in the works by 1998. Pohlad, the billionaire head of a banking empire, had a checkered business history in the Twin Cities, including experience with profiting from the public till. After he was tapped by the state in 1959 to head up a bus company that had been brought to the brink of bankruptcy under the control of local mobsters, Pohlad wound up cutting bus maintenance and pension-fund payments, demanding a fare increase despite turning profits—and siphoning off at least $4 million in interest-free loans to help buy the Tropicana Casino in Las Vegas. Pohlad was later part of Frank Lorenzo's scandal-plagued management of Eastern and Continental Airlines in the 1980s. Through all this,

his family fortune, which began when he took control of a local bank in the 1940s, soared to more than $1 billion.[12]

The opposition to a new Twins ballpark was unusually well organized from the start. Jon Commers, a former state legislative aide, launched Fans Advocating Intelligent Spending out of the offices of a local progressive activist group. Along with Ricky Rask's Fund Kids First, Commers set out to muster public opposition to Pohlad's demands, focusing particular attention on the 18 state legislators who had sworn during the 1996 election campaign not to spend public money on a new stadium.

On the Twins' side, meanwhile, was only one prominent politician: Governor Arne Carlson.

Proclaiming himself the state's "number one fan," Carlson is an unabashed rooter for all of Minnesota's sports teams and has expressed an interest in becoming a sports booster when he retires from public office; he once called a press conference to criticize the officiating at a college basketball game. So when the Twins came looking for an ally, the state's highest public official was more than happy to jump on board. Asked once why Pohlad couldn't spend his own money on a stadium, Carlson snapped, "That's irrelevant," and accused people opposed to subsidizing billionaires of promulgating "class warfare."[13]

In January, Pohlad and Henry Savelkoul of the Metropolitan Sports Facilities Commission proudly announced that they had a plan that would satisfy everyone. The state would spend $277.5 million toward a $360 million stadium with a retractable dome; in exchange, Pohlad would give the people of Minnesota ownership of 49 percent of the team. At the time, Major League Baseball had a stated policy against against public ownership of any portion of a franchise, which would mean opening their secret bookkeeping to public scrutiny, but this didn't stop the plan from being hailed by *Star Tribune* sports columnist Sid Hartman as a marvel of generosity: "Never has the owner of a football or base-ball team offered a package such as the $158 million gift and 49 percent interest in the team that Twins owner Carl Pohlad has offered the state."[14]

On January 26, the first polls came in—and they gave Carlson's plan a resounding thumbs-down. Fully 69 percent of Minnesotans said they opposed the deal; even self-identi-fied Twins fans were slightly inclined toward opposition. When asked to list public spending priorities in order of importance, those polled ranked pro sports dead last.[15] Worse yet for the Twins, the *St. Paul Pioneer-Press* reported that Pohlad's $82.5 million "contribution" to the stadium—not $158 million, as Hartman had erroneously reported—would in fact be a loan, not a gift, one that he expected to be paid back should he sell the team. The Twins quickly backpedaled, claiming that calling it a gift had been a "mis-communication," but the damage was done.

From there, the Twins quickly stepped up their campaign. The consulting firm Arthur Anderson was hired to produce a glowing report on the economic benefits of a new ballpark. Pohlad began to make more overt threats to move the team elsewhere if his demands weren't met, though skeptics won-dered whether the cities rumored as destinations for the ball-club—which included such metropolises as Charlotte, North Carolina, and Portland, Oregon, the home of the Twins' top minor-league team—would bring him any more revenue than he was already getting in Minnesota.

The team also tried to leverage the star power of its players, parading Kirby Puckett, a local hero whose Hall of Fame career was cut short by glaucoma, around the state to stump for a new ballpark. Although some Minnesotans resented what they con-sidered Puckett's prostituting himself for a new baseball stadium, one state senator who Puckett and other Twins stars had lobbied defended the visits, asserting that "it's not unlike when you want to pass the victim's rights bill, you bring in the victim."

He paused, then added, "That's not a good analogy."[16]

...Lose a Few

Meanwhile, the Twins and state couldn't even agree on a price tag. The cost of the new ballpark—with retractable roof, of course—fluctuated wildly between $300 million and $500 million over the course of the winter.

Public opinion remained unenthusiastic—a citizen's panel brought together by the *Star Tribune* and a local TV station unanimously gave the deal a thumbs-down. "If I invest two-thirds of the money, I want more than 49 percent," said retired lab technician Bob Koebele. And Deb McNeill, a store manager who supported the stadium before the forum, announced that she had changed her mind: "I grew up thinking of the Twins not as a business, but more as a public entity. But the team isn't. They are a business. I'm not able to defend public funding. I have nothing to defend it with."[17]

With the public ownership option going nowhere—one sports commission member declared it "dead as a smelt"—Carlson turned to more likely prospects for revenue. First, the governor suggested a ten-cents-a-pack cigarette tax, earmarking nine cents for stadium construction and one cent for anti-smoking programs; that bombed with public health advocates, who asked why all ten cents shouldn't be devoted to public health. Finally, a bill was introduced to place slot machines at a local racetrack, which its legislative sponsor optimistically predicted would generate $50 million a year for the state—raising an outcry from the state Indian reservations that relied on casino revenue to fund their own budgets. "If ever someone gets around to writing a brochure on 'How a Bill *Doesn't* Become Law,'" the *Star Tribune* concluded, "the author might use the proposed Twins stadium as a case study."[18]

The clock finally ran out on May 19, as the state legislature closed its session without voting on a stadium bill. Six months later, it reconvened in special session to once again consider stadium options. This time, there was an immediate threat on the table: In October, Pohlad had signed a deal to sell the Twins to North Carolina businessman Don Beaver, who would move it to that state's Triad region (Greensboro, High Point, and Winston-Salem). The deal would be called off only if the legislature approved a stadium funding bill by November 30.

The bill that was finally submitted for legislative approval was a bizarre hodgepodge of different proposals. Under this plan, Pohlad would give the team to a non-profit foundation, which would pay off his $86 million in accrued debts by selling it to another local owner within five years; Pohlad would also earn a substantial tax break on the "charitable contribution" of his team, valued at $140 million, to the foundation. The state, meanwhile, would pay the entire cost of building a $404 million stadium, this time via an all-new funding scheme: redirecting income taxes and sales taxes from the stadium to pay off the construction bonds. (A similar mechanism, known as "tax increment financing," is commonly granted by cities to private developers in other industries.) Proponents argued that this was no different from other fees, such as hunting licenses, that were earmarked for specific purposes; critics pointed out that as these funds would otherwise go into the state's general fund, this was as direct a subsidy as there could be. "The financing of the thing is too screwy," one *Star Tribune* reader wrote to the paper's website, noting that if players' income taxes could be used to pay for a stadium, "I think my income tax should go towards improving the place I work."[19]

Legislators, by and large, agreed; the tax-increment scheme garnered little support. At the last minute, stadium proponents frantically tried to fashion a different bill that would pay for the new stadium entirely with "user fees"—profits on the future sale of the Twins by the foundation, higher parking and sales taxes at the ballpark, plus surcharges on player salaries and sports broadcasts. But even as the baseball players union and local broadcasters screamed bloody murder, that plan ran into a still more imposing obstacle: the money raised wouldn't be nearly enough to pay construction costs. A new stadium, just as Robert Baade and his fellow economists had predicted, couldn't pay its own way.

The calls that poured in to the capitol switchboard were running 3-2 against stadium funding; Minneapolis voters, meanwhile, overwhelmingly approved a $10 million cap on city funding of any new ballpark. Finally, on November 13, the legislature threw in the towel, with the House voting 87-47 to reject the last-ditch proposal, then adjourning the special session for good. "On November 13, professional baseball died in Minnesota," proclaimed House stadium bill sponsor Loren Jennings.[20]

Yet Pohlad, who had earlier insisted that his sale of the team would kick in if the legislature adjourned without passing a stadium bill, still hesitated. "Everybody says it's dead," he said after the House vote. "I don't know if it is or not."[21] The November 30 deadline passed with the future of the Twins, and the stadium, still undecided.

San Francisco: If At First You Don't Succeed...

San Francisco's history with sports owner demands has been particularly epic—involving "10 years, five mayors, four referenda, four cities, and one earthquake," as one observer put it.[22] It began in 1984, when then-San Francisco Giants owner Bob Lurie, who had bought the team eight years earlier to prevent it from being moved to Toronto, declared that he would sell the team to out-of-town interests if he didn't get a new stadium. Candlestick Park, the team's home since moving west from New York in 1958, was best known as the coldest and windiest place in the Bay Area (Giants pitcher Stu Miller was once blown off the mound by a gust of wind), and Lurie was determined to get a replacement at public expense.

San Francisco, however, has a very different means of approving public expenditures than most U.S. cities. Virtually all city bond issues must be subject to approval by the electorate (this was true even before Proposition 218 passed new statewide restrictions on issuing bonds in 1996), meaning the Giants would have to subject their stadium demands to a public referendum.

The first such referendum was Proposition W, in 1987, which called for an $85 million stadium in the South of Market warehouse district. Held during a mayoral election in which three of the four candidates opposed the initiative, it went down to a 53 percent to 47 percent defeat. Two years later, having swayed new Mayor Art Agnos to climb aboard the stadium bandwagon, the Giants tried again with Proposition P. By this time, the price tag had risen to $115 million, the site had shifted several blocks to the San Francisco waterfront—and the margin of defeat was one percent, helped along by an electorate more concerned with rebuilding from the previous month's earthquake than with upgrading a ballpark that had remained standing throughout the temblor, beneath the feet of 60,000 fans waiting for a World Series game to begin.

The following year, Lurie tried a new strategy: Sick of San Francisco voters, he pitched a multi-city funding effort to build a new stadium south of San Francisco, near San Jose. This time, the Giants managed to win one vote—but lost three others, sending the complicated funding scheme down to defeat. In 1992, yet another referendum, this one limited to San Jose, crashed and burned, as 55 percent of city voters declined to hand over $185 million in utility taxes for a new ballpark.

Every time Lurie had come back to the public asking for money—more and more money each time, in fact—he had presented the upcoming vote as the "last hope" of keeping the Giants in the Bay Area, and it was understandable if the citizenry was beginning to suspect that the move threat wasn't all it was cracked up to be. But then Bob Lurie did what no baseball owner had done in 20 years: He sold his team to a group of investors from the Tampa Bay area. The team, it was announced, would begin play in Florida in 1993. Finally, it seemed, an owner had been pushed too far; without public subsidies, you really couldn't guarantee that a sports team would stay put, even in a populous area like San Francisco.

The National League owners voted to reject the sale.

The reasons were complex. A Giants move might help spread fear in other cities faced with pending stadium legislation, but it would also take Tampa Bay out of the running as a locale for other teams to move to—as several teams were then threatening to do. The San Francisco Bay Area was the nation's fifth-largest TV market; Tampa Bay ranked 14th, meaning a potential loss of network TV revenue for the whole league when the national broadcast contract came up for renegotiation. And finally, there was a local ownership group, led by Safeway supermarket magnate Peter Magowan, ready to buy the team and keep it in San Francisco, albeit at a slightly lower price than what the Tampa Bay group was offering. The league told Lurie to take the Magowan bid; Lurie took it. All those referenda, it turned out, hadn't been the last hope of retaining the Giants, but merely the last hope of retaining Bob Lurie.

Magowan immediately set out to secure the new ballpark that Lurie had failed to get, with one major difference: This time, the Giants were prepared the foot the bill themselves. The Giants would build and own the planned $255 million waterfront ballpark, with almost the entire cost paid for out of a private bond issue and the sale of naming rights and luxury boxes. Proposition B passed in May 1996 by a two-to-one margin, and the Giants at last had their ballpark.

The San Francisco story to this point has become near-legendary among anti-stadium activists: the little electorate that could, calling the bluff of the leagues and getting to keep their team and their money, too. Even the $1.2 million a year in hidden subsidies later approved for Magowan's privately funded ballpark (for relocating a Port of San Francisco maintenance yard on the same China Basin site rejected in the 1989 referendum), or the $15 million in public tax increment financing (in which the city would divert property taxes on the land into the construction fund) didn't dim enthusiasm: The Giants were still building the first privately funded baseball stadium in three decades, largely because voters had indicated loud and clear that they had no intention of footing the bill.

Such qualms would pale, though, in comparison to the next demand placed before the San Francisco electorate. The Giants had a co-tenant at Candlestick Park: the immensely popular 49ers football team. And 49ers owner Eddie DeBartolo had decided it was time to cash in on the sports welfare gold rush.

Mall in the Family

The 49ers management set out to prove that, done right, even the most anti-subsidy city in the U.S. could be forced to cough up money for a new stadium. Then they proceeded to do almost everything wrong.

The first rumblings came in late 1996, as the aftershocks of the previous year's move of the Cleveland Browns to Baltimore and the announced shift of the Houston Oilers to Tennessee were still echoing in the ears of football fans. Team owner Edward DeBartolo, a multimillionaire real estate developer, warned that the team, which had turned a $19 million profit in 1995—tops among NFL teams—and was fresh from its fifth Super Bowl victory in 14 years, could no longer field a "competitive" team without the help of a new stadium. "Given the fact that there are many cities that would build them a new stadium at no cost, it's a real tribute that the 49ers have moved from asking the city for money to looking for some kind of alternative," said Jack Davis, who the 49ers hired to lead their campaign for a new stadium.[23]

Davis and the 49ers didn't look very hard. By February 1997, the team was asking for $100 million in public subsidies for a new stadium on the Candlestick Park site. The referendum—actually two referenda, Propositions D and F, one to approve the funding and the other to ease zoning restrictions—would go before the voters in June.

The first thing DeBartolo and Policy did was to insist (as the Miami Heat had in their campaign for a "waterfront park" the previous year) that they weren't really asking for a stadium at all. The new 49ers stadium, they announced, would be but a mere portion of a planned mall development to be built by Mills Corp. If eight days of football a year—plus the three Super Bowls over the next 30 years that NFL commissioner Paul Tagliabue was dangling as an incentive for the city to build a new stadium—wouldn't generate enough economic activity to make the public investment worthwhile, what of a giant shopping mall, drawing consumers from all over the region? And where $100 million might look like a lot to invest in a $325 million stadium, it would be a mere fraction of the cost of a $525 million "entertainment complex."

"For every $4.25 that the 49ers put on the table," Davis told the press, "the city puts $1, and the dollar is not a dollar that comes out of the budget for police and fire. When the public takes a look at the deal, it's clearly and convincingly about jobs and economic opportunity."[24]

The first member of the public to take a close look at the numbers disagreed. On February 7, San Francisco Board of Supervisors budget analyst Harvey Rose released a study claiming to show that the city would lose $4.6 million a year on the new stadium, and possibly more if the megamall drew off shoppers from other retail outlets in the city.[25] City controller Ed

Harrington promptly issued a competing report claiming that the new mall "should generate new revenues sufficient to pay all, or a substantial portion of" the construction costs—and Harrington's report, unlike Rose's, would be included in the official city voter guide for the referendum.[26]

The next obstacle for the team came from the stadium's opponents. The anti-49ers campaign was being led by Joel Ventresca, a veteran of the successful fights against subsidizing the Giants, but it was a pair of local individuals who would cause the biggest uproar. Taking advantage of a San Francisco law allowing residents to buy space in the city voter guide to argue for or against ballot measures, the pair paid $269 for a satirical ad *in favor* of the stadium project. "Opponents call it 'Candlestick Pork' and 'corporate welfare,'" wrote local attorney Dan Larkosh and self-proclaimed "aspiring millionaire" John Hlinko. "Perhaps. But when you're from Ohio, making money in San Francisco means expensive flights, paying for dual housekeeping staffs, limo drivers, etc. This adds up!" Larkosh signed the missive, "Multimillionaires for Corporate Welfare." Critics charged the pair with making a "laughingstock" of the election; Larkosh responded, "If the truth is funny, so be it."[27] The ad wound up being kicked into the "con" section of the voter guide, but not before the ensuing public uproar had introduced millions of area newspaper readers to the arguments within.

The biggest fiasco of all, though, was brought on by the 49ers' campaign director himself. DeBartolo was determined to keep himself and his $600 million net worth out of the limelight, and club president Carmen Policy was less than silver-tongued with the public. (In first announcing the team's desire for a city-funded stadium the previous fall, Policy had declaimed, "Once the mayor gets into the posture where he believes and sees you're not trying to milk the cow dry, but only enough to fill the glass so you don't choke on the cookies, can we proceed."[28]) So the team hired Jack Davis, a well-known local political operative who had managed the Giants' referendum campaign the year before, to make their case before the voters.

Davis looked like the perfect choice for the job. A former campaign director for Mayor Brown and other prominent area politicians, he kept a low personal profile while pushing the 49ers' stadium project at every opportunity. Until, that is, May 3, when Davis threw himself a 50th birthday party to which he invited Mayor Brown, 49ers president Policy, and other local luminaries. That wasn't the story; the entertainment was: a performance artist who, dressed in a Native American headdress, had a colleague carve a satanic star into his back, urinate on him, and sodomize him with a whiskey bottle.

It was hardly the sort of thing the team wanted associated with its PR specialist. "The Party" dominated headlines for days, with reaction ranging from ridicule to outrage. Denni Woodward, director of Stanford University's American Indian and Alaska Native Program, summed up the performance as "combining [an indigenous culture] with some kind of cheap horror movie. I think he's probably offended everybody from the Apache Mescalero to the Satanists."[29]

The 49ers responded with a flurry of new promises in an attempt to drive the Davis party uproar from the front pages. One day, the team was announcing that it would provide health benefits to domestic partners of gay employees; another, it was taking out an insurance policy (a legally toothless one, it turned out) against the city having to pay any money out of general funds. The new stadium, it was promised, would provide jobs for the impoverished residents of nearby Hunters Point. By the end, DeBartolo himself had entered the fray, defending the stadium deal with every argument he could muster.

"Candlestick is almost to the point where it'll be condemned," he told a group of undecided women at a "For Women Only" pro-stadium event in May. To renovate it, he insisted, "would cost too much—$180 million."

"Is that your estimate or someone else's?" asked one woman.

"Look, you'd be throwing good money after bad," DeBartolo replied. "The key thing is the economic benefit to the city. People don't understand why the mall is there, but it's the engine that runs the train."[30]

Going into the June 3 vote, public expectation was that the two propositions would go down in defeat, just like the four attempts by the Giants at public funding. The team's threats to take the team to hated rival Los Angeles had been met more with derision than concern: "Threatening to go to Los Angeles is like holding a gun to your own head and threatening to kill the hostage," quipped one newspaper columnist.[31] The last poll, taken two weeks before the election, had shown the stadium initiative trailing by nine percentage points, with little sign of change during the months of lobbying by the team and the mayor.

Instead, it squeaked to victory by a little more than a thousand votes. Huge margins of victory in Hunter's Point led to allegations of voter fraud, especially after it was reported that polls had been opened at city-run housing projects in that neighborhood several days before election day. City employees, it was further revealed, had been pressured ("encouraged," insisted the mayor's press secretary) into taking off the day of the election to do pro-stadium campaigning.[32]

The deal, however, was done. After spending more than $2 million on the pro-stadium campaign—$33 per yes vote—including $1.25 million of DeBartolo's family fortune, the 49ers had their stadium.[33] "The guy upstairs must really have wanted for this to happen," exclaimed Policy at a jubilant post-election party for the 49ers and their backers.[34]

Presumably, he wasn't talking about DeBartolo.

The Stadium Merry-Go-Round

In June 1997, *Your Money* magazine ran a list of all the major-league baseball, football, and basketball franchises and their stadiums and arenas; an asterisk marked each team that was seeking a new building. Out of 74 teams, there were 29 asterisks: from the Boston Red Sox to the San Diego Padres, the Sacramento Kings to the Charlotte Hornets. And that didn't include the 21 teams already playing in new or newly renovated facilities; or the 14 that had new buildings under construction. It also left out an entire country (Canada) and major sport (hockey), which would have accounted for perhaps a dozen more stadiums and arenas, in progress or under negotiation.[35]

Despite all the concrete that has already been poured, the new stadium craze shows no signs of abating—in fact, it has spread to such places as England and Australia, where publicly funded soccer stadiums increasingly dot the landscape. In North America, there are more stadiums and arenas going up each year than at any time in history. The sports industry seems to be settling into an equilibrium where at any given time, one quarter of major-league teams are playing in new buildings, one quarter are awaiting their construction, yet another quarter are lobbying to get them built—and a final quarter is waiting in the wings for their turn at the plate. And once those teams have gotten their new toys, it will be time for the last round of stadium-beggars to line up again for another handout, for their stadiums will be slipping into "economic obsolescence."

"If you go into building a new stadium now and aren't prepared for major changes by that second decade," Mark Rosentraub told the *Minneapolis Star Tribune* in the midst of the Twins fight, "you're being Pollyannaish about it."[36] As San Franciscans can attest, if you *don't* build a new stadium now, just wait a couple of years—someone will doubtless make a new pitch for one then.

10 THE BUCKS STOP HERE

"The loyal rooters never doubted for a moment that their beloved Bums were as much a part of their heritage as Prospect Park. They discovered they were wrong. The Dodgers were only a piece of merchandise that passed from hand to hand."
—BASEBALL OWNER BILL VEECK[1]

When Cleveland Indians outfielder Albert Belle left the team, and the city, for a huge contract with the rival Chicago White Sox in the spring of 1997, Cleveland fans were outraged. (They showed it by greeting him with a chorus of boos and obscene gestures when he returned to Jacobs Field to play as a member of the visiting team.) It was as if in leaving the Indians Belle had betrayed his citywide extended family—a family that had been extorted by its own parents to fork over hard-earned dollars to keep the team in town by paying for a new stadium.

If They Don't Win It's a Shame

For generations, the special emotional presence of the local team has been played up—by sports promoters, by the local media, by fans themselves. These are home teams: unique, regional representations of a city's heart and soul. The intensity of the connection between local fan and hometown team has divided family loyalties, driven real estate decisions, and dominated debate at countless dinner tables.

Decades later, there are still New Yorkers who have never recovered from the awful day in 1957 when Walter O'Malley abruptly yanked the Brooklyn Dodgers out of Ebbets Field and moved them 3,000 miles to Los Angeles. There are grown men and women who walked away from baseball fandom that day and never looked back, others who switched allegiance to the crosstown Yankees or Giants, still others who raised their children on Brooklyn lore—reminiscing about a long-gone franchise. The Dodgers were a neighborhood team, they represented a proud if increasingly struggling urban community, and they were as much a part of daily life as the local churches or recreation centers. The bond was a real one—at least from the point of view of the fans.

How important is that relationship? When major league baseball was hit by financial disputes and labor unrest in the early and mid-1990s, one of the great fears heard among sports marketers and commentators alike was about the alienation of fans. What would happen to the sport's popularity, it was wondered, when fans thought of the ballclubs as collections of free agent millionaire athletes looking out for their own financial best interests before the good of their team—thus willing to leave Americans without their beloved baseball in the interest of higher salaries? And what would happen when fans thought of professional owners as similarly self-interested billionaires—willing to shut down America's pastime before agreeing to player demands, willing to search for more hospitable climes when local municipalities couldn't produce sparkling new diamonds? It's a concern that pops up periodically, among sports journalists and bottom-line network presidents, among professional sports leagues and hot-stove league fans. What would happen, in other words, when the myth of home teams belonging, emotionally, morally even, to home cities was exploded in the face of faithful fans?

What happened, apparently, was a great deal of sound and fury without any clear significance. Major league baseball attendance dropped, but it had already been on a downward trend. For years, league officials have bemoaned the difficulties of bringing America's youth back to the game. Of course, that occasional disinterest on the part of the country's future consumers may have just as much to do with overpriced seats and concession items, fancy new stadiums with distant views, and the increasing popularity of other sports as with a realization that there isn't any guaranteed "home" in your hometown baseball club. But still, the warning was out—beware the alienation of the fan, beware the cynicism of the consumer. The myth of public participation in local professional sports needed to be as strong as ever, in order to prevent further declines in fan interest and avoid threats to franchise profits.

Out of the Mouths of Legislators

But what *are* concerned citizens supposed to do if their sports team is threatening to leave town unless it gets a publicly funded new stadium? Sympathetic to the plight of sports fans who don't want to lose their team or shell out large amounts of tax dollars, some legislators have tried to find a solution through the law. Unfortunately, these approaches do not offer a readily apparent way out of the problem.

The main focus of legislative efforts to put the brakes on stadium subsidies thus far has been a bill sponsored by New York Senator Daniel Patrick Moynihan. Nearly all activists speak of it with some hope, and perhaps not surprisingly, nearly everyone at the recent Sports Facilities Finance Conference spoke with some apprehension about the Moynihan bill.

Picking up from where the 1986 Tax Reform Act fell short, the Moynihan-sponsored Stop Tax-exempt Arena Debt Issuance Act (STADIA) would essentially rule out altogether the use of federally tax-exempt bonds for any pro sports facilities.

However, by late 1997 the bill had few sponsors. And even if it were to somehow pass, it was likely to have exemptions tacked on by members of Congress seeking special projects in their districts.

Furthermore, the Moynihan bill won't stop stadium construction, just raise the cost of capital. Cities would be under pressure to sell taxable, rather than tax-exempt, bonds. Since they carry higher interest rates, these bonds end up costing much more. An extra two percent a year—the standard difference in rates—on $400 million in bonds would amount to $8 million per year in extra costs to the local government issuing the bonds. The problem is that that two percent extra interest is a lot of money, because these bonds usually have a long maturity. If they mature in three years, the extra $24 million might not seem that much—less than six percent of the actual cost. But if they mature in 20 years, the extra interest would amount to $160 million, or well over a third of the cost. The Moynihan bill could easily end up just shifting this part of the subsidy from the federal government to local governments.

There have been other recent attempts at federal legislation as well. Oregon Representative Earl Blumenauer has proposed a bill saying that in order to keep congressionally granted monopoly privileges, leagues would have to allow municipal ownership and would have to give current cities first dibs on buying teams before the owners can move them. Ohio Representative Martin Hoke introduced a similar bill in 1996, only to have it "lobbied to death by the NFL's hired guns," a Hoke staffer told *U.S. News and World Report*.[2]

Other activists have tried devising various means of stopping corporate welfare in general. Corporate welfare activists like Greg LeRoy have proposed various "clawback" provisions (where states get money back if the promised jobs aren't created), as well as multi-state commissions to develop regional no-competition pacts among states. They sound promising enough, but some other corporate welfare opponents (notably Arthur Rolnick of the Minneapolis Federal Reserve) don't see them going anywhere—clawbacks are only as good as the will to enforce them. (For example, a clawback law was in place with Northwest Airlines, but the state of Minnesota later renegotiated it to avoid alienating the airline company.) Additionally, every attempt at a regional commission so far has fallen apart when one of the parties gets the opportunity to steal a plum business from another locality.

Rolnick instead has a proposal that, he insists, would stop corporate welfare in its tracks: Have the IRS tax corporate welfare as imputed income. In other words, if your state builds you a $400 million stadium, you have to declare $400 million income on your taxes. Needless to say, this would greatly reduce the incentive for companies to seek corporate welfare.

Rolnick says he's had numerous legal experts look into the possibility of such a law, and he is certain it's constitutional. He thinks it compares favorably with interstate agreements to stop corporate welfare, since, as he says, the Compact Clause of the Constitution "really doesn't allow states to make contracts like this—that's what you've got Congress for."

Whether this is politically feasible is another story. One would think that Congress would have no interest in maintaining local corporations—why should the federal government care where in the United States a company is located—but, of course, Congress itself is made up of locally elected politicians, who have the same ties to corporations and dependence on their campaign contributions and the like as local politicians. In 1997, Minnesota representative David Minge introduced a federal bill to levy a 35% excise tax on local government subsidies, but it likely faces an uphill battle in Congress.[3]

Bringing 'em Home

There is one other solution that has been suggested for stadium subsidies. It's one that would tap into the very mythology that pro owners use when trying to persuade local populaces to build them new stadiums. It's always about "our" team, after all, at least according to the owners' public relations flacks—about our town and our pride. In the spring of 1985, when the Cleveland Indians were facing yet another ignominious season on the playing field and the city itself was being asked to build a new stadium to keep the team in town, someone in the club's public relations office came up with an appropriate catchphrase to drum up support for the new baseball season. "Tribe '85," went the saying, printed on bumper stickers and pins, home game giveaway items and local advertising, "This Is My Team!"

But what if it really *were* our team?

When the world champion Chicago Bulls basketball team takes the court before each sold-out game at the United Center, they are often presented by the dramatic public address announcer as "your Chicago Bulls." But what if they really were?

When Clevelanders heard Art Modell was pulling the Browns out of town, they were stunned. These were the Cleveland Browns; they weren't Art Modell's to pick up and scatter whichever way the financial windfalls blew. They belonged to the town as much as Lake Erie and pierogis, battles over school desegregation and deindustrialization, didn't they?

Amid the demands for petition drives and rallies were few calls for one obvious solution. They were the Cleveland Browns, after all. Why not have the city buy the team? One group, at least, saw it as an easy choice: "The state, county, or city of Berea, where the Browns Corp. is located, can legally take over the team. Modell can be paid off later but the team will stay," read an Ohio Communist Party flyer handed out at local rallies. "You, the greatest fans in the world, can make this happen....Get your union, church, or community group to speak out in favor of public takeover of the Browns through eminent domain."

And really, the demand seemed fairly straightforward. If they belonged to the city, the Browns would still be packing 'em in at Municipal Stadium. Winter Sunday afternoons would still mean big crowds at corner taverns, paper dog bones pasted into store windows, GO BROWNS spelled out across corporate vistas. Why *shouldn't* the team belong to the city?

After all, hasn't it worked for the Green Bay Packers for nearly 50 years?

Well, yes and no. The Packers, though often cited as a "publicly owned" team by the media, are not actually owned by the municipality of Green Bay, but neither are they run by a single private owner. In 1950, when the Green Bay Packers football team was on the verge of bankruptcy, the team went public as a non-profit corporation, with about 5,000 shares of stock at $25 apiece. The team now has 1,915 stockholders (mostly Wisconsin residents, but also citizens from every state and three foreign countries)—none of whom have ever received dividends. Instead, profits are directed back into the franchise. Ownership bylaws prohibit any individual from holding more than 200 shares; if stockholders want to sell, they must first go to the board of directors' executive committee. That committee decides if it will buy the shares back or reissue them. And so for decades the team and its unique ownership group have wrestled with the big issues in modern sports—the executive committee spurned the chance to build a dome over hallowed Lambeau Field, but authorized the addition of luxury boxes. The wait for season tickets is in the tens of thousands, and the city has long been renowned for its enthusiastic embrace of the team.[4]

Public Is as Public Does

Like corporate heads recognizing the public relations value in "partnerships" with potential unionized employees, team owners have risen to the challenge in recent years and talked about putting teams more in "public" hands. Their recent method of choice? Team owners have mimicked the situation in Green

Bay, but only in the most superficial sense, by making public offerings of millions of shares of stock in the ball clubs—but only as much as 49 percent of the club, leaving the team firmly in private control. Given that *public* is so often a dirty word in the contemporary U.S. corporate lexicon, and that its authentic meaning would challenge the fundamental interests of the very private owners of sports teams, the only acceptable role for the public is as Wall Street traders.

Both the Boston Celtics, the historic basketball team, and the Florida Panthers, an expansion hockey franchise, are publicly traded. Panthers owner Wayne Huizenga apparently decided to make the public offering, in November 1996, to bring in even more money for his billion-dollar coffers. Huizenga, the former Blockbuster Video owner whose holdings also include the Florida Marlins baseball team, maintains control of the team, making the public offering a purely symbolic—and potentially fruitful—gesture. (He sold 49 percent of the common stock, but retains other, non-trading stock for himself.) "I don't think the institutionals will touch this," David Menlow, the president of IPO Financial Network, told the *Fort Lauderdale Sun-Sentinel* at the time. "This is a nostalgia buy rather than an investment."[5] But with a minimum $1,000 investment, Huizenga stands to profit off that nostalgic gesture. And the fans themselves, those who think they're buying a true stake in their hometown team's fortunes, are in for a rude surprise. "If the pattern of previous publicly traded teams holds," according to *The Wall Street Journal*, "most Panthers certificates will end up hanging on barroom walls, given as birthday presents or the like."[6]

The Celtics, which became the first team to go public when they did so in 1986, have seen below-average stock performance since that move.[7] But that initial offering also gave the team's owners a windfall profit of some $48 million.[8] "On the one hand, you can say [the Celtics are] the exception," says sports economist Rodney Fort. "On the other hand, you can say, so what if they're publicly traded? Nothing is really different about the Celtics than any other team. Because, after all, if you issue lots of stock in little bitty bunches, and you maintain the majority of the stock, then who cares?"

The most recent attempt to ease public concerns by offering publicly traded shares came from the Minnesota Twins. And though Twins owner Carl Pohlad's offer of 49 percent stock in the team caused the local press to declare it would be "essentially creating a partnership between the Pohlad family, who owns the Twins, and the state of Minnesota," apparently nobody else in the state was fooled enough to drum up support.[9] When it became clear that the locals weren't going to be taken in, Pohlad withdrew the offer.

But what about actual municipal ownership? Some cities, when confronted with jittery owners threatening to skip town, have attempted to utilize their right to eminent domain—the governmental right to take over private property (including land) for public use. They tried it in Oakland, when the Raiders football team announced it was fleeing to Los Angeles in 1980, and the city attempted to seize the club by eminent domain. The California Supreme Court rejected the case on the grounds that the seizure would "impermissably burden interstate commerce."[10] Public officials had even less luck in Baltimore when the city tried to prevent the Colts from leaving town; that team's middle-of-the-night flight to Indianapolis took place before the city could make its case in court.

But what if a city had a chance to buy or own a professional sports team, without having to claim it through eminent domain? It's been done at the minor-league level with baseball teams in New York and Ohio, as well as in the Canadian Football League. And it almost happened in major league baseball with the San Diego Padres.

When Joan Kroc inherited ownership of the San Diego Padres baseball team in 1984 from her husband, the late

McDonald's founder Ray Kroc, she had little interest in baseball as a sport or the team as a franchise. But the multimillionaire's mind was changed when she saw how the Southern California community supported its local ball club, and she became convinced that the Padres should truly belong to their hometown.[11]

So the philanthropic heiress, who would in 1997 make headlines by giving out thousands of dollars apiece to flood victims in the Midwest, made the city of San Diego an offer it truly couldn't refuse: She wanted to give the team to the city, and include a $100 million trust fund in order for the city to operate it. San Diego Mayor Maureen O'Connor greeted the offer with delight and enthusiasm, as did other city officials. It would have kept the team in San Diego, rid it forever of ugly ownership battles, and provided the capital to attempt a management structure.

It seemed too good to be true, and it was. Because when Kroc took her suggestion to the owners committee of Major League Baseball, they refused to even consider it.[12] A truly publicly owned team apparently would have meant a huge headache—if nothing else, by opening up the heavily guarded major league financial books to public scrutiny.

"If the city owned it, we would have it in perpetuity, and that is obviously the best of all worlds," O'Connor told the *San Diego Union-Tribune*. "I was sick, personally, when it didn't come off, because with a $100 million trust fund,... it would have been great.... I can tell you I was very sad when they turned her down."[13]

The events in San Diego—and in Montreal, where the Expos ownership had wanted to sell the team to a public/private interest that included the province of Quebec—were a harsh reminder that professional sports teams do not exist to foster the public good.[14] They might have the names of cities on them (at least for now, although a more honest approach might follow the lead of Japanese baseball teams and call them the Steinbrenner

Yankees, the Turner Braves, and so on) but, despite owner claims to the contrary, they are profit-making machines like few others—and no right-thinking for-profit owner would want anything to tamper with his or her set-up.[15] "Think about the way owners deal with cities now, with an artificial maintenance of scarcity of teams," says Rodney Fort. "You can't lose in that situation: 'Give me what I want, or I'll split.' Well now, if the city decided to keep a marginally valuable franchise hanging around, to keep a minority of potential voters happy, then the value of your league goes down. They'll never do it in 10,000 years."

There was briefly, in the early 1990s, an attempt by economist Andrew Zimbalist, sports agent Richard Moss, and others to create a competing professional baseball league, the United Baseball League, that would have teams owned by consortia of players, municipalities, and private investors. Mike Stone, the former president of the Texas Rangers, was to be the proposed league's first CEO. Citing the league's unique philosophy as what drew him in, he said in a 1995 interview that "baseball should be a partnership among owners, then between owners and players, between franchises and communities, and between franchises and their fans."[16]

In the UBL, cities would actually have received some revenue. And teams would have pooled half their television and radio revenues, as well as 30 percent of their gate receipts. Initial hopes were to have teams in Florida, Puerto Rico, New York, and Washington, D.C., in its Eastern Division, and Los Angeles, Portland, Vancouver, and New Orleans in its Western Division. The hope was to have play begin in 1997, but when an all-important promised TV contract fell through a year earlier, the league officially suspended operation.

If Only

If sports teams were municipally owned, sports stadiums would not be nearly as expensive to build. Existing structures wouldn't have to be razed to satisfy an eager owner's desire to see team profits or his own net worth rapidly increase. Instead, cooler heads might prevail when changes in architecture or money-making cause some to cast a longing eye toward sparkling new facilities. For if they aren't inherently cooler-headed, local politicians at least have some democratic accountability to local taxpayers—something corporate owners are sorely lacking.

"It's a logical thing to happen," says Zimbalist. "Sports teams are just perfect vehicles for public ownership for all sorts of reasons—the most important being the large investment the public is expected to make in these teams, but also because it's really a public good, and it has a cultural dominance that's unlike anything else in our society."

True municipal ownership might have to mean a radical rearranging of our society, and a significant challenge to powerful interests who will not stand passively by and let this happen. To bring this public good—i.e., the ball clubs that are invested not only with public money but with public spirit as well—under public control raises broad issues about how other resources are to be managed in our society.

When Seattle attorney Shawn Newman went to testify in the spring of 1997 before state senate hearings on publicly funding a new stadium for the Seahawks, he had one crucial point to make. "I said the bottom line is that a lot of people out in the audience have T-shirts on which say, 'It's our team. It's our team.' And I said, 'It's not our team. It is Paul Allen's team, or it's this Ken Barron, the bad developer's, team. It's not our team.

"State law, believe it or not, would allow us to buy the damn team. Counties or cities can buy the team. I talked to the governor's lobbyists over here, and he said we can't do that, we can't buy the team, because the NFL has changed the rules. No more Green Bay Packers—you can't do that anymore. So it's not our team. What it is, it's our debt."

AFTERWORD: WINNING ISN'T EVERYTHING

Seattle activist Chris Van Dyk has noticed a new term emerge in civic debates in his town. When it's time to discuss budget issues or policy decisions, a relatively new expression is thrown around. When the merit of supporting a new project arises, concerned taxpayers or city council members now ask, "Is it a More Important Thing?"

A little over two years of furious lobbying and petitioning, granting media interviews and suing as part of opposition to two stadium deals did not produce victory for Citizens for More Important Things. But their impact on the political vocabulary in Seattle suggests that they had a real, if modest, impact on consciousness there.

So did the Cleveland Teachers Union (CTU) and other opponents of out-of-control tax abatements in Cleveland. In a town that had seen three new publicly funded stadiums authorized in six years, they succeeded, in the summer of 1997, in getting a public vote on the future of tax abatements. It was one of the only times in memory that a community group had brought the way corporate construction projects are typically financed nationwide onto the table for discussion. That measure ultimately lost, but not before receiving national media attention—including a glowing endorsement in USA Today—and having an impact on the way people in that city talk about stadiums and schools. Indeed, in the midst of their collective bargaining battle a year earlier, the CTU threatened to march from each major symbol of tax abatement and opportunities lost for the Cleveland schools—Jacobs Field, the downtown Tower City shopping mall—to City Hall. And, in a significant departure from most economic struggles, which tend to be defined in very narrow terms, in that 1996 campaign the CTU successfully projected the connection between public spending on sports boondoggles, tax abatements, low teacher salaries, and poor service to their pupils. When the administration learned through polling that the teachers had won widespread public support, their once-resolute opposition collapsed and they yielded, allowing the CTU to win a historic agreement.

The lessons to be learned from all the stadium battles past and present are complex. The money, media, and resources behind team owners and local politicians make them formidable opponents, and their winning streak in getting new stadiums is impressive. But the terms of debate are changing, even if so far the teams have consistently won the arguments. Politicians must be increasingly careful to appear to stand up to owner greed—witness Cleveland Mayor Michael White's attempt to lead the opposition to Art Modell's pulling the Browns out of Cleveland at the same time he was speaking out on holding down costs in the construction of the new football stadium. The fact that White's rhetoric seems to many observers both insincere and misplaced does not change the fact that as an astute politician he felt he had to take an anti-owner stance in response to changes in popular thinking.

Team owners must devise increasingly devious and manipulative ways of gaining access to the public's wealth to finance their new sports facilities. The popularity of personal seat licenses, naming rights deals, and roundabout tax financing schemes are no coincidence—they've come about because owners and their political allies have learned that many city residents don't want publicly funded new stadiums. More newspaper and magazine articles are written exposing the stadium swindle, while fewer people now take seriously the argument that funding sports stadiums is good business for city governments.

There's a tendency, particularly in the sports world, to frame success in terms of winners and losers. Yet the "losses" for the grassroots anti-stadium campaigns—and for the schools, the public housing, all the public amenities that are forced to go without when corporate welfare is made a priority of public spending—only point to how necessary these types of campaigns are. When a multimillionaire sports team owner can sway politicians, buy elections, and con the public all through the power of the purse, what better sign that something drastic needs to happen to change the balance of power in our society?

For the activists fighting block by block and referendum by referendum to put an end to sports subsidies, seeking small victories in the larger defeats has become a familiar pursuit. "Moral victories are wonderful, but I'd still rather win the election," says Seattle's Van Dyk with a laugh.

In *Captain Newman, M.D.*, his classic novel of American GIs during World War II, Leo Rosten writes of the importance of people's ability to hold onto important values while resisting seemingly overwhelming forces. He addresses both the dignity of undertaking apparently quixotic struggles, and the necessity of working for meaningful and winnable change.

What if Destiny came down to an island community, Rosten asks, and told the inhabitants they'd be inundated by a tidal wave tomorrow? Rosten's wise man responds that he'd study how to live underwater. "I too never forgot that story," his Captain Newman says. "When our cause seems doomed and the future lost, when despair becomes unbearable, and the heart is on the edge of breaking, let men summon hope and honor and high resolve in yet one more stubborn affirmation: Come let us assemble our wisest men and begin at once to think, to study, to try to learn—even to learn, if we must, how to live underwater."[1]

The effective blackmail that professional teams wield over cities is not good, it is not correct, and it is not eternal. It is the consequence of a particular state of affairs in which public agencies have become beholden to private power. It can be changed, and it's worth changing.

NOTES

NOTE: *All unsourced quotations are taken from interviews conducted by the authors between February 1996 and October 1997.*

Chapter 1

1. Peter Richmond, *Ballpark*. New York: Simon & Schuster, 1993, p. 97.
2. Robert McG. Thomas Jr., "Colts' Move to Indianapolis Is Announced." *The New York Times*, March 30, 1984.
3. Dave Anderson, "12 Vans to Indianapolis." *The New York Times*, April 1, 1984.
4. Jacob V. Lamar Jr. and Don Winbush, "'India-no-place' No More; The subject of a joke gains major league attention." *Time*, June 11, 1984.
5. Andrew H. Malcolm, "The Colts' Move: For Indianapolis It's a Boon…But in Baltimore, It Leaves a Void in the Hearts of the Fans." *The New York Times*, April 8, 1984. Kent McDill, "Why is Indianapolis building a $75 million domed stadium?" UPI, June 27, 1982.
6. The Raiders' ultimately successful lawsuit challenged the NFL's right to control franchise movement; until it was resolved, the league put its expansion plans on hold. (Mark Fury, "Will Indianapolis' Domed Stadium Become a White Elephant?" *Bond Buyer*, July 28, 1982.)
7. Fury, "Will Indianapolis' Domed Stadium Become a White Elephant?"
8. Charles C. Euchner, *Playing the Field: Why Sports Teams Move and Cities Fight to Keep Them*. Baltimore: Johns Hopkins University Press, 1993, p. 105.
9. According to Hudnut's chief negotiator, the deal was finalized in just three days because of fears of legal entanglements. ("Rushed negotiations for Colts revealed," UPI, April 1, 1984.)
10. "Most Modern Stadium in the World, and One of Most Beautiful." *The Plain Dealer*, July 31, 1931.
11. Carol Poh Miller and Robert Wheeler, *Cleveland: A Concise History, 1796-1990*. Bloomington: Indiana University Press, 1990, p. 143.
12. Local baseball fans, desperately searching for explanations for one of the most ignominious reputations in professional sports history, were willing to turn to any explanation. Besides the stadium's inhospitability, Clevelanders pointed to the legendary "curse" of Rocky Colavito, the popular Indians outfielder who was inexplicably traded before the start of the 1960 season. (Terry Pluto, *The Curse of Rocky Colavito*, New York: Simon and Schuster, 1994, p. 47.)
13. Poh Miller and Wheeler, *Cleveland: A Concise History*, pp. 183-184.

14.   Mark Rosentraub, *Major League Losers: The Real Cost of Sports and Who's Paying for Them.* New York: BasicBooks, 1997, p. 256.

15.   "All it took was a significant proportion of the political elites to contest it," says Elkins, who points out that even Voinovich "had to be persuaded and cajoled." In the course of his own research on the domed saga, Elkins spoke with Campanella and many of the other key figures.

16.   Paul Attner, "For Many Cities, There's No Place Like Dome." *The Washington Post*, June 8, 1994.

17.   Elkins also speculates that there may have been a greater than normal turnout by African-American voters on that day in May 1984—it was the same election day that would see Jesse Jackson score significant numbers in the city of Cleveland in his presidential campaign.

18.   Poh Miller and Wheeler, *Cleveland: A Concise History*, p. 189.

19.   Richmond, *Ballpark*, p. 49.

20.   Richmond, *Ballpark*, p. 58.

21.   Euchner, *Playing the Field*, p. 115.

22.   Richmond, *Ballpark*, p. 96.

23.   That the warehouse was owned by Schaefer's chief fundraiser was, no doubt, merely coincidence. (Euchner, *Playing the Field*, p. 115.)

24.   Richmond, *Ballpark*, p. 44.

25.   Rosentraub, *Major League Losers*, p. 256. In Rosentraub's extensive look at stadium financing and the cost to local municipalities, he argues that the Jacobs brothers were seen as the ideal new owners of the beleaguered team. Rebuilding the Indians was part of the brothers' plans for redeveloping downtown Cleveland.

26.   Ibid., p. 263.

27.   Emphasis in original. Newspaper advertisement, *The Plain Dealer*, May 3, 1990.

28.   Roldo Bartimole, "If you build it." *The Progressive*, June 1994.

29.   Rosentraub, *Major League Losers*, p. 261.

30.   Ibid., p. 263.

31.   Ibid., pp. 269-278.

32.   "Gateway agrees to pay taxes on Jacobs Field, Gund Arena." James F. Sweeney, *The Plain Dealer*, December 24, 1996.

33.   Perhaps it should have been. In *Ballpark*, Peter Richmond mentions, almost in passing, that in 1984 then-Baltimore Mayor William Schaefer "mobilized a secret meeting...between [Orioles owner Edward] Williams, Governor Hughes, Cleveland Browns owner Art Modell, and Larry Lucchino. It was Schaefer's idea: the state would donate the land, private capital would be raised, and Art Modell, a friend of Williams,

would buy an NFL team, put it in Cleveland, and move his Browns in."
(Richmond, *Ballpark*, p. 65)

34. Stephen Koff, Timothy Heider, and Evelyn Theiss, "How Cleveland lost the Browns." *The Plain Dealer*, November 19, 1995.

35. Malcolm Moran, "Hugs, Tears and a Victory: Browns Say Goodbye." *The New York Times*, December 18, 1995.

36. Tom Cushman, "Maybe S.D. deal with Chargers is not so bad." *San Diego Union-Tribune*, November 17, 1995.

37. Stephen Koff and Tony Grossi, "City may need new stadium to keep a team, NFL says." *The Plain Dealer*, January 5, 1996.

38. Ibid.

39. *The Plain Dealer*, February 11, 1996.

40. Norman Krumholtz, "To fund or not to fund?" *Detroit Free Press*, March 12, 1996. W. Dennis Keating, "Cleveland: The Comeback City." Mickey Lauria, ed., *Reconstructing Urban Regime Theory: Regulating Urban Politics in a Global Economy*, Thousand Oaks, Calif.: Sage, 1997, p. 192.

41. Sandra Dallas, ed., "Tackling Football, And Oh, Yes, Education," *Business Week*, December 9, 1996.

42. Scott Stephens, "Cleveland schools to cut sports, teachers," *The Plain Dealer*, March 8, 1996.

43. According to Jack Lapides, the poorest 25 percent of the state's population buys 63 percent of all lottery tickets. (Richmond, *Ballpark*, p. 98.)

44. Though the Maryland Stadium Authority would later rent out office space in the warehouse to local companies, as a state agency it pays no property taxes. Jack Lapides reports that over his three decades in the state senate, the portion of city land not paying property taxes had nearly doubled, from 20 percent to 37 percent, as a result of the sports stadiums, university and hospital expansion, and other tax-exempt development.

45. John Helyar, *Lords of the Realm*. New York: Ballantine Books, 1994, pp. 569-572.

46. www.financialworld.com.

Chapter 2

1. John Williams, "Early stadium sketches unveiled." *Houston Chronicle*, October 12, 1996.

2. John Riley, "Where the Grass Is Always…Greener: An $8.1B building boom in pro-team stadiums: How public money is fueling private fortunes." *Newsday*, August 18, 1996.

3. James Quirk and Rodney Fort, *Pay Dirt*. Princeton, N.J.: Princeton University Press, 1992, p. 127.

4.   Kary L. Moss, "The Privatizing of Public Wealth." *Fordham Urban Law Journal*, XXIII:1, 1995, p. 106.
5.   Greg LeRoy, "No More Candy Store." Federation for Industrial Retention and Renewal and Grassroots Policy Project, 1994, p. 3.
6.   Ibid.
7.   Phil Bereano and Todd Fedorenko, "High Tech Candy Store." *The Seattle Times*, March 23, 1997.
8.   Moss, "The Privatizing of Public Wealth," p. 107.
9.   John Butera, "The Ties That Bind." *Plants, Sites and Parks Magazine*, March/April 1996.
10.   Janice Shields, "Ending Corporate Welfare," *Business and Society Review*, Summer 1995.
11.   Greg LeRoy, *No More Candy Store*, p. 2.
12.   Mark Rosentraub, *Major League Losers: The Real Cost of Sports and Who's Paying for Them*. New York: BasicBooks, 1997, pp. 66-67.
13.   Mark Thornton, "Bring Back the Football Cartel." *The Free Market*, January 1996.
14.   Andrew H. Malcolm, "The Colts' Move…For Indianapolis It's a Boon….But in Baltimore It Leaves a Void in the Hearts of the Fans." *The New York Times*, April 8, 1984.
15.   Charles C. Euchner, *Playing the Field: Why Sports Teams Move and Cities Fight to Keep Them*. Baltimore: Johns Hopkins University Press, 1993, p. 55.
16.   Richard Sandomir, "Mayor Says if Yanks Must Move, West Side Would Be Best," *The New York Times*, April 3, 1996.
17.   Robert A. Baade, "Stadiums, Professional Sports, and Economic Development: Assessing the Reality." A Heartland Policy Study, April 4, 1984.
18.   Ibid.
19.   Joanna Cagan and Neil deMause, "The great stadium swindle." *In These Times*, August 19, 1996.
20.   Steers, "Bowlen for Dollars."
21.   Rosentraub, *Major League Losers*, pp. 151-153.
22.   Terry Fiedler, "Boosters: Ballpark would aid economy." *Minneapolis Star Tribune*, March 4, 1997.
23.   Rosentraub, *Major League Losers*, pp. 138-149.
24.   Euchner, *Playing the Field, p.* 67.
25.   Dennis Zimmerman, "Tax-Exempt Bonds and the Economics of Professional Sports Stadiums." Congressional Research Service, May 29, 1996.

Chapter 3

1.   Andrew Zimbalist, *Baseball and Billions* (Updated Edition). New York: Basic Books, 1994, p. 62.
2.   Michael K. Ozanian, "Value Investing, Sports Division." *Financial World*, May 20, 1996, p. 70.
3.   A year later, Raleigh, North Carolina beat out Nashville, luring the Whalers with a $120 million publicly funded arena.
4.   Charles C. Euchner, *Playing the Field: Why Sports Teams Move and Cities Fight to Keep Them*. Baltimore: Johns Hopkins University Press, 1993, p. 65.
5.   James Quirk and Rodney Fort, *Pay Dirt*. Princeton, N.J.: Princeton University Press, 1992, pp. 56-63.
6.   Quirk and Fort, *Pay Dirt*, p. 209.
7.   John Helyar, *Lords of the Realm*. New York: Ballantine Books, 1994, p. 249.
8.   Bill Veeck, *Veeck as in Wreck*. New York: Ballantine Books, 1976, pp. 173-178.
9.   Zimbalist, *Baseball and Billions*, p. 65.
10. Ibid., pp. 65, 215.
11. Helyar, *Lords of the Realm*, p. 347.
12. Quirk and Fort, *Pay Dirt*, p. 97.
13. Daniel Patrick Moynihan, *Congressional Record*, January 25, 1997.
14. Jeff Wilkinson, "Marketing guru upbeat over seat applications." *Nashville Banner*, January 1, 1996.
15. Ibid.
16. Robert Hennelly, "Field of Schemes." *Village Voice*, October 5, 1993.
17. Celeste Hadrick, "Arena Face-Off." *Newsday*, August 21, 1996. Robert Fresca, "Teams Play Hardball." *Newsday*, August 21, 1996.
18. Since some of the expenditures will be deferred many years, this amounts to roughly $525 million in current dollars.

Chapter 4

1.   John Riley, "Where the Grass Is Always…Greener: An $8.1B building boom in pro-team stadiums: How public money is fueling private fortunes." *Newsday*, August 18, 1996.
2.   John Williams, "Users to pay a majority of stadium costs." *Houston Chronicle*, October 20, 1996.
3.   Riley, "Where the Grass Is Always…Greener."
4.   Michael Betzold and Ethan Casey, *Queen of Diamonds*. West Bloomfield, Michigan: Altwerger and Mandel, 1992, pp. 137-139.
5.   Paul Attner, "For Many Cities, There's No Place Like a Dome." *Washington Post*, June 8, 1984.

6.   Like Comiskey, Metropolitan Stadium for years had been undermaintained; one account called it "the most poorly maintained park in the Majors," where broken railings created a safety hazard in 1981, just before the Twins moved into the Metrodome. See www.ballparks.com.

7.   Christopher Lopez and Jeffrey A. Roberts, "Are new arenas worth it? Broncos, Nuggets are going on offensive for new digs." *Denver Post*, August 14, 1994. As of mid-1997, the Nuggets and their co-tenants, the Colorado Avalanche hockey franchise, were awaiting word on their proposed multimillion-dollar publicly financed Pepsi Center.

8.   Stuart Steers, "Bowlen for Dollars." *Denver Westword*, December 20, 1995.

9.   Lopez and Roberts, "Are new arenas worth it?"

10. Steers, "Bowlen for Dollars."

11. John Pastier, "Diamonds in the Rough." *Slate*, July 31, 1996.

12. Kevin Mulligan, "Lurie: Birds staying at least in the area." *Philadelphia Daily News*, July 23, 1996.

13. Phillip Matier & Andrew Ross, "Chastened 49ers Own Up to Unsportsmanlike Conduct." *San Francisco Chronicle*, February 12, 1997.

14. Steinbrenner's lawyer in the campaign contribution case: future Orioles owner Edward Bennett Williams. (Ed Linn, *Steinbrenner's Yankees*. New York: Holt, Rinehart and Winston, 1982, p. 48.)

15. John Williams, "Baseball officials want Houston to hurry stadium plans." *Houston Chronicle*, August 8, 1996.

16. Jay Weiner, "Bud Selig addresses Minnesota Legislature on stadium." *Minneapolis Star Tribune*, May 1, 1997.

17. Associated Press, May 6, 1997.

18. Alan Truex, "Threat of Astros moving to Virginia remains alive." *Houston Chronicle*, June 19, 1996.

19. So named because an enterprising local registered a trademark to the preferred name, the Stingrays, and refused to let it go for less than a small fortune.

20. Jay Weiner, "Few cities either ready or willing to adopt Twins." *Minneapolis Star Tribune*, May 12, 1997.

21. Bill Steigerwald, "Phoenix's Diamond in the Sun." *Pittsburgh Post-Gazette*, June 12, 1997.

22. John Williams, "Astros debt list is huge." *Houston Chronicle*, August 15, 1996.

23. *Financial World*, June 17, 1997.

24. Donald L. Henry, "On the Move." *Business Facilities*, April 1996.

25. Edward Epstein and John King, "49ers' Deal Raises Doubts." *San Francisco Chronicle*, February 8, 1997. John King, "Controller's Message

to Voters Boosts 49ers Stadium Measure." *San Francisco Chronicle*, March 20, 1997.

26. John Williams and Terry Blount, "Officials pitch idea of ticket drive to save Astros." *Houston Chronicle*, October 20, 1995.

27. Mark Rosentraub, *Major League Losers: The Real Cost of Sports and Who's Paying for Them*. New York: BasicBooks, 1997, pp. 321. Betzold and Casey, *Queen of Diamonds*, pp. 214, 242-243.

28. David Brauer, "Let the Stadium Wars Begin." *Citypages*, April 1996.

29. Jonathan D. Silver, "Bombshell Provided New Stadium for Brewers." *Pittsburgh Post-Gazette*, June 2, 1997.

30. Kenneth R. Lamke and Amy Rinard, "Stadium funding plan revived." *Milwaukee Journal Sentinel*, June 10, 1996.

31. Kenneth R. Lamke, "As deals go, Brewers' is in middle." *Milwaukee Journal Sentinel*, August 12, 1996.

32. Brauer, "Let the Stadium Wars Begin." In November 1997, the stadium cost estimate was revised upwards by an additional $50 million, leaving the state still further in the hole. (Jim Chilsen, "Brewers park may cost $50 million more." Associated Press, November 13, 1997.)

33. Stephanie Salter, "The 49ers need a new game plan." *San Francisco Examiner*, June 1, 1997.

Chapter 5

1.   Paul Ferrante, "Save Our Stadium!" *Sports Collectors Digest*, September 20, 1996.

2.   The Tigers won, 2-1, with rookie catcher Matt Nokes breaking up the opposing team's no-hitter with a two-run single in the bottom of the 9th.

3.   Michael Betzold and Ethan Casey, *Queen of Diamonds*. West Bloomfield, Michigan: Altwerger and Mandel, 1992, pp. 109-110. Betzold and Casey's history of Tiger Stadium and the first five years of the Tiger Stadium Fan Club is easily the most comprehensive case study of a stadium scam to date and was invaluable in compiling this chapter.

4.   *Unobstructed Views: The Tiger Stadium Fan Club Newsletter*, February 1988, p. 1.

5.   Betzold and Casey, *Queen of Diamonds*, p. 126.

6.   Ibid., p. 132.

7.   Ibid., p. 134.

8.   Ibid., pp. 149-150.

9.   *Unobstructed Views*, Summer 1988, p. 1.

10. Betzold and Casey, *Queen of Diamonds*, p. 154.

11. John Pastier, "Diamonds in the Rough." *Slate*, July 31, 1996.

12. Betzold and Casey, *Queen of Diamonds*, p. 154.

13. Ibid., p. 155.
14. Ibid., p. 157.
15. Ibid., p. 157.
16. Ibid., pp. 209-210.
17. Ibid., p. 145.
18. *Unobstructed Views*, November 1995, p. 1.
19. Associated Press, March 22, 1996.
20. Valarie Basheda, Shawn Lewis and Phil Linsalata, "Voters like pitch, OK stadium funding." *Detroit News*, March 20, 1996.
21. Jeffrey Chadiha, "Baseball struggles to get minorities interested again." *San Francisco Examiner*, June 15, 1997.
22. V. Lonnie Peek, Jr., "Stadium Support Strengthens." *Michigan Chronicle*, February 14-20, 1996.
23. Tom Henderson, "Chuck Forbes: Mad as Hell But Forced to Take It." *Corporate Detroit*, January 1997. Moten later left city government and went to work for Little Caesar's.

Chapter 6

1. Bill Steigerwald, "Phoenix's Diamond in the Sun," *Pittsburgh Post-Gazette*, June 12, 1997.
2. Edward Epstein, "Brown Says 'Trust Me' On Stadium," *San Francisco Chronicle*, February 26, 1997.
3. John Carman, "Radio Gets Mayor's Mouthful," *San Francisco Chronicle*, June 5, 1997.
4. Carla Marinucci and Gregory Lewis, "Foes say team spent $33 a vote to carpet bomb City." *San Francisco Examiner*, June 4, 1997.
5. Murphy also served on the presidential campaigns of George Bush in 1988 and 1992, and Bob Dole in 1996.
6. *Minneapolis Star Tribune* editorial, June 6, 1997.
7. Joanna Cagan and Neil deMause, "Root, Root, Root for the Home Team." *Extra!*, August 1996.
8. Eric Brazil, "49ers drive toward goal as clock ticks down," *San Francisco Examiner*, June 1, 1997.
9. Scott Ostler, "Brown Wins With His Jabbing." *San Francisco Chronicle*, June 2, 1997.
10. Beth Hawkins, "Home Field Advantage." *Minneapolis City Pages*, April 2, 1997.
11. Ibid.
12. Michael Francher, *The Seattle Times*, September 24, 1995.
13. All quotes in this section from California Newsreel's *Fear and Favor in the Newsroom*, 1997.

14. O. Casey Carr, "The Civic Power Brokers No One Elected." *The Seattle Times*, April 2, 1997.
15. Ibid.
16. Ibid.
17. David Schaefer and David Postman, "Stadium measure is passing." *The Seattle Times*, June 18, 1997.

Chapter 7

1. Charles C. Euchner, *Playing the Field: Why Sports Teams Move and Cities Fight to Keep Them*. Baltimore: Johns Hopkins University Press, 1993, pp. 133-159.
2. Doug Bukowski, *Baseball Palace of the World*. Chicago: Lyceum Books, 1992, p. 12.
3. Ibid, p. 9.
4. Douglas Bukowski, Mary O'Connell, John Aranza, "Comiskey Park: A Landmark Proposal," Save Our Sox, Chicago, Illinois, 1987, p. 16.
5. Bukowski, *Baseball Palace of the World*, p. 86.
6. Ibid., p. 18.
7. Ibid., p. 4.
8. Euchner, *Playing the Field*, pp. 133-159. Euchner cites a market study the new owners had done in the early 1980s, which urged the team to develop a strong suburban fan base; he also looks to the television broadcasting wars with the North Side Cubs and the general trend in the '70s and '80s to locate key parts of Chicago industry away from the inner city and in the area's growing suburban sprawl.
9. Bukowski, *Baseball Palace of the World*, p. 4.
10. Ibid.
11. Ibid.
12. Ibid.
13. John J. Betancur, Michael Leachman, Anne Miller, David Walker, Patricia A. Wright, "Development Without Displacement," Task Force Background Paper, The Chicago Rehab Network, The Nathalie P. Voorhees Center for Neighborhood and Community Improvement, June 1995. Euchner, *Playing the Field*, p. 154.
14. Ibid.
15. Kenneth L. Shropshire, *The Sports Franchise Game*. Philadelphia: University of Pennsylvania Press, 1995, p. 11.
16. *Unobstructed Views*, May 1995, p. 4.
17. Philip J. Lowry, *Green Cathedrals*. Reading, Mass.: Addison-Wesley, 1992, pp. 49-50.
18. Andrew Zimbalist, *Baseball and Billions*. New York: Basic Books, 1992, p.129

19.   John Helyar, *Lords of the Realm*. New York: Ballantine Books, 1994, p. 483.

20.   Bukowski, *Baseball Palace of the World*, p. 17.

Chapter 8

1.   Philip Bess, "Urban Ballparks and the Future of Cities." *Real Estate Issues*, December 1996.

2.   Leonard Pitts Jr., "'…a professional football team is far more important than 30 libraries.'" *The Baltimore Sun*, August 30, 1996.

3.   Philip Bess, "City Baseball Magic." *Minneapolis Review of Baseball*, 1989, p. 25.

4.   James Tackach and Joshua B. Stein, *The Fields of Summer*. New York: Crescent Books, 1992, p. 67.

5.   Philip J. Lowry, *Green Cathedrals*. Reading, Mass.: Addison-Wesley, 1992, pp. 11, 191.

6.   Ibid., p. 4.

7.   Ibid., p. 4.

8.   James Quirk and Rodney Fort, *Pay Dirt*. Princeton, N.J.: Princeton University Press, 1992, p. 162.

9.   Charles C. Euchner, *Playing the Field*. Baltimore: Johns Hopkins Press, 1993, pp. 156-7.

10.   M. Christine Boyer, "Cities for Sale: Merchandising History at South Street Seaport." Michael Sorkin, ed., *Variations on a Theme Park*, New York: Hill and Wang, 1992, p. 181-204.

11.   Russ Rymer, "Back to the Future." *Harper's*, October 1996.

12.   Ibid.

13.   Robert Whereatt, "Public unmoved by Twins' proposal," *Minneapolis Star Tribune*, January 26, 1997.

14.   W. Dennis Keating, "Cleveland: The Comeback City." Mickey Lauria, ed., *Reconstructing Urban Regime Theory: Regulating Urban Politics in a Global Economy*, Thousand Oaks, Calif.: Sage, 1997, p. 192.

15.   "How Much Does It Really Cost." *Critique*, February 1997.

16.   Tamar Lewin, "Seeking to Shield Schools From Tax Breaks." *The New York Times*, May 21, 1997.

17.   There are numerous excellent studies on the policy of structural adjustment and its impact on the developing world. Among them, see Osvaldo Sunkel, "Economic reform and democratic viability" in Joseph S. Tulchin, ed. *The Consolidation of Democracy in Latin America* (Boulder: Lynne Rienner, 1995). He suggests that Latin American democratization is going to be undermined by neoliberal economic reform. Also, Isabella Bakker, ed., *The Strategic Silence: Gender and Economic Policy* (London: Zed Books, 1994). And Kerianne Piester,

"Targeting the Poor: The politics of social policy reforms in Mexico" in Douglas A. Chalmers, Carlos M. Vilas, Katherine Hite, Scott B. Martin, Kerianne Piester, and Monique Segarra, eds., *The New Politics of Inequality in Latin America: Rethinking Participation and Representation* (Oxford: Oxford University Press, 1997).

18. Steve Cagan, "Our Stadium." WCPN-FM commentary, May 6, 1997.

Chapter 9

1. Robert Whereatt, "Public unmoved by Twins' proposal." *Minnesota Star Tribune*, January 26, 1997.
2. "Chronology: The Long Goodbye." *The Seattle Times*, December 15, 1996.
3. O. Casey Corr, "Ballpark's a big pain—and proud of it." *The Seattle Times*, April 2, 1997.
4. "Last Out for Baseball in Seattle, Excerpts of Owners' Statement." *The Seattle Times*, December 15, 1996.
5. Ericy Pyrne and O. Casey Corr, "Seattle Holding Firm on Stadium Deal." *The Seattle Times*, December 25, 1996.
6. Ibid.
7. "Locke: Let state vote on stadium funding tax aimed at aiding Hawks." *The Seattle Times*, February 21, 1997.
8. Carey Goldberg, "Billionaire Finances a Vote About Replacing a Stadium." *The New York Times*, May 25, 1997.
9. Robert Fresco, "Teams Play Hardball." *Newsday*, August 21, 1996.
10. Jay Weiner, "Lessons learned from Target Center." *Minneapolis Star Tribune*, May 7, 1997.
11. Janice Shields, "Ending (Corporate) Welfare As We Know It." *Business & Society Review*, Summer 1995.
12. Chris Ison and Paul McEnroe, "Dealing with Carl Pohlad." *Minneapolis Star Tribune*, April 20, 1997.
13. Jay Weiner, "State's First Fan talks about sports and a new stadium." *Minneapolis Star Tribune*, December 1, 1996.
14. Beth Hawkins, "Home Field Advantage." *Minneapolis City Pages*, April 2, 1997.
15. Robert Whereatt, "Public unmoved by Twins' proposal." *Minnesota Star Tribune*, January 26, 1997.
16. Robert Whereatt, "Twins legends make pitch for ballpark." *Minneapolis Star Tribune*, March 11, 1997.
17. Jay Weiner, "Citizen panel says 'no' to funding new Twins stadium." *Minneapolis Star Tribune*, January 23, 1997.
18. Robert Whereatt, "The rise (and fall) of the Twins ballpark bill." *Minneapolis Star Tribune*, March 10, 1997.
19. Michael T. Johnson, post to www.startribune.com, November 10, 1997.

20. Conrad deFiebre, Jay Weiner, Robert Whereatt and Dane Smith, "Out at home: Legislators vote down 'final' stadium plan." *Minneapolis Star Tribune*, November 14, 1997.

21. Ibid.

22. John Yewell, "Build It Yourself, Carl." *Twin Cities Reader*, March 5-11, 1997. The Giants chronology that follows is drawn largely from Yewell's article.

23. Phillip Matier and Andrew Ross, "Public Opposes Paying for 49er Stadium." *San Francisco Chronicle*, October 28, 1996.

24. Susan Yoachum and Edward Epstein, "Stadium Poll Holds Lessons For 49ers." *San Francisco Chronicle*, March 11, 1997.

25. Edward Epstein and John King, "49ers' Deal Raises Doubts." *San Francisco Chronicle*, February 8, 1997.

26. John King, "Controller's Message to Voters Boosts 49ers Stadium Measure." *San Francisco Chronicle*, March 20, 1997.

27. Edward Epstein, "Ballot Satirists Hauled Into Court." *San Francisco Chronicle*, April 2, 1997.

28. Edward Epstein, "49ers Want Taxpayers to Help Carry the Ball for New Stadium." *San Francisco Chronicle*, September 10, 1996.

29. Michael Dougan and Julie Chao, "Raunchy 'Ritual.'" *San Francisco Examiner*, May 8, 1997.

30. Joan Ryan, "49ers Woo Women's Vote With Wine, Words—And Steve Young." *San Francisco Chronicle*, May 16, 1997.

31. Rob Morse, "49ers 90210? Like, I'm so sure." *San Francisco Examiner*, May 22, 1997.

32. Michael Howerton, "Winning ugly: How Willie Brown used city employees to win the 49ers stadium-mall." *San Francisco Bay Guardian*, June 11, 1997.

33. Carla Marinucci and Gregory Lewis, "Foes say team spent $33 a vote to carpet bomb City." *San Francisco Examiner*, June 4, 1997. Eric Brazil, "Funding the Stadium Fight." *San Francisco Examiner*, May 23, 1997.

34. Gwen Knapp, "In the end, sentiment led to 'ugly' win." *San Francisco Examiner*, June 4, 1997.

35. Deborah A. Rogus, "America's Sports Stadiums: How Much Do They Really Cost You?" *Your Money*, June/July 1997.

36. Jay Weiner, "Is The Dome Doomed?" *Minneapolis Star Tribune*, April 28, 1997.

Chapter 10

1. Bill Veeck, *The Hustler's Handbook*. New York: G.P. Putnam's Sons, 1965, p. 305.

2. Jason Vest, "Uproot for the home team." *U.S. News and World Report*, March 10, 1997.

3. Mike Meyers, "Minge bill puts subsidy debate on national agenda." *Minneapolis Star Tribune*, December 3, 1997.

4. Johnette Howard, "Frozen in Time." *Sports Illustrated*, January 13, 1997.

5. Larry Lebowitz, "Investors go for Panthers Shares; analysts warn of potential losses," *The Fort Lauderdale Sun-Sentinel*, November 14, 1996.

6. Ed Fowler, "Franchise owners too rich for their own good," *Houston Chronicle*, September 29, 1996.

7. Ibid.

8. Joanna Cagan and Neil deMause, "Buy the bums out." *In These Times*, December 9, 1996.

9. "Twins announce plans for new outdoor ballpark." January 8, 1997, Minnesota Twins Team News, Minnesota Twins/Major League Baseball Web site.

10. Cagan and deMause, "Buy the bums out."

11. Barry Lorge, "Kroc Wanted to Give Padres to City; Owners' Committee Thwarted Philanthropic 1989 Offer." *San Diego Union-Tribune*, July 29, 1990.

12. Ibid.

13. Ibid.

14. Kenneth L. Shropshire, *The Sports Franchise Game*. Philadelphia: University of Pennsylvania Press, 1995, p. 62.

15. Major league owners did vote, in September 1997, to allow for public stock offerings in professional baseball teams, but the gesture seems likely to be as ultimately meaningless as it is in the other major sports.

16. Ross Atkin, "Move Over Major Leaguers, Here comes the UBL." *Christian Science Monitor*, September 29, 1995.

Afterword

1. Leo Rosten, *Captain Newman, M.D.* New York: Harper & Row, 1961, p. 331.

INDEX

ACKNOWLEDGMENTS

Before this book was a book, before it was even a gleam in our publisher's eye, it was supposed to be a cute little 1,000-word article on the irony of cities spending money on sports stadiums while squeezing their own citizens. That article, published in the political zine *Brooklyn Metro Times*, quickly grew into a 4,200-word behemoth, and our thanks go out to our fellow zinesters who helped tame that beast for publication: Nina Ascoly, Max Freund, Kurt Gottschalk, Bernie McAleer, and Michelle Phipps. Likewise, great thanks to Jim Naureckas, editor of *Extra!*, and Deidre McFayden, executive editor of *In These Times*, for their invaluable support in crafting the articles that helped lead to this book.

This book also would not have been possible without our tireless crew of informants, who barraged us with a steady stream of news clippings from farflung stadium battles: Ted Benson, Rob Daviau, Janet Pope, and Wendy Roth. Likewise, we owe a great debt of thanks to the time, wisdom and expertise shared with us by the grassroots activists, academics, and researchers who were extremely generous in sharing their time and information with us. Our thanks to: Hallie Amey, John Aranza, Robert Baade, Roldo Bartimole, Philip Bess, Doug Bukowski, Michael Charney, Jon Commers, John Davids, Judy Davids, Dorothy Dean, David R. Elkins, Rodney Fort, Meryl T. Johnson, Dennis Keating, Norman Krumholtz, Greg LeRoy, Bill Marker, Marge Misak, Shawn Newman, Mary O'Connell, Kevin O'Brien, John Pastier, Frank Rashid, Sheila Radford-Hill, John Ryan, Janice Shields, Kim Stroud, Newton Suewe, Hank Trenkle, Chris Van Dyk, and Andrew Zimbalist.

We also benefitted tremendously from a group of friends and colleagues who shared their editorial and critical skills throughout the formation of the book. Our thanks to: Eileen

Mullin, Mindy Nass, Jim Naureckas, Nancy Nisselbaum, Andrew Ross, Anne Savarese, and Misha Tepper. Margot Abel, Peet Cenedella, and Wendy Roth provided invaluable assistance with the introductory chapters, as did Beth and Steve Cagan with the final ones.

Finally, it was Greg Bates at Common Courage Press who first approached us with the idea of turning our articles on the great stadium swindle into a book—our thanks to him for that (we think) and to him and Liz Keith for their constant support for and belief in this project.

Joanna writes: In a crazy and stressful year, this book was only possible because of the tireless enthusiasm and support of friends and family. My thanks to Jennifer Eaton, Miles Seligman, Regina Shields and Jeanette Valentine—I wouldn't have survived without their timely meals and free clipping services, their excellent couch-sitting abilities, their patience when other parts of life were frequently disrupted and, most importantly, their unwavering faith in me and this project even when I didn't have much of either. Likewise, the long-distance advice, camaraderie and frequently tested sob-proof skills of Susan Snyder and Lisa Tozzi were simply invaluable, as was the constant cheerleading of Jessie and Shauna Cagan. I would be remiss if I didn't also thank Craig Campanella for an impeccably timed email and Lisa Sklar for her daily enthusiasm. And finally, to my parents Beth and Steve Cagan—who offered endless advice, patience, humor and compassion when I needed them all. Thanks for showing me the way.

Neil writes: I'd like to thank my friends and family for keeping me sane throughout the writing of this book—unfortunately, my sanity left me somewhere around Chapter Two, so I can't do that. Instead, let me present a hearty helping of thanks to: Matthew Amster-Burton, Adam Cadre, Liza Daly, Rob Daviau, and all the denizens of rec.arts.int-fiction who kept me in good humor throughout this project; the members of the Echo writing conference who helped kibitz the title into shape; Echo itself, for the Net access I never knew how much I needed (did people really write books before AltaVista?); everyone at Fairness and Accuracy In Reporting, for generosity of both time and resources; Jeff Kisseloff, who reassured me that all books take forever to write and twice that to rewrite; Peet Cenedella, Eileen Mullin, Wendy Roth, and all my other friends kind enough to answer the phone at midnight to calm my anguished mind; Quinn, Cleo, and Lucy, for lap-sitting above and beyond the call of duty (they're cats, okay?); and, most of all, Mindy Nass, for her wisdom, clarity, humor, and above all patience for a partner inclined to disappear at odd moments into the computer. I couldn't have done it without you.

ABOUT THE AUTHORS

A long-suffering Cleveland sports fan, JOANNA CAGAN has umpired little-league baseball, been denied access to the Syracuse lockerroom for postgame interviews and judged a pageant for male cover models. She's also written for the *Village Voice*, *In These Times*, *Extra!* and *Brooklyn Metro Times*.

NEIL DEMAUSE is a regular contributor to *In These Times*, *Extra!*, and *Z* magazine, among other progressive publications, and a co-founder of the political zine *Brooklyn Metro Times*. He has personally witnessed four World Series games, two no-hitters, and the death of New Deal liberalism.

For further information and news updates on sports stadiums and corporate welfare, visit the *Field of Schemes* website at http://www.echonyc.com/~neild/fieldofschemes/